Geronimo: Prisoner of Lies
Twenty-Three Years as a Prisoner of War, 1886–1909

W. Michael Farmer

TWODOT®

GUILFORD, CONNECTICUT
HELENA, MONTANA

A · TWODOT® · BOOK

An imprint and registered trademark of The Rowman & Littlefield Publishing Group, Inc.
4501 Forbes Blvd., Ste. 200
Lanham, MD 20706
www.rowman.com

Distributed by NATIONAL BOOK NETWORK

British Library Cataloguing in Publication Information available

Library of Congress Cataloging-in-Publication Data available

ISBN 978-1-4930-4200-5 (hardcover)
ISBN 978-1-4930-4201-2 (e-book)

∞™ The paper used in this publication meets the minimum requirements of American National Standard for Information Sciences—Permanence of Paper for Printed Library Materials, ANSI/ NISO Z39.48-1992.

Printed in the United States of America

For Corky, my best friend and wife

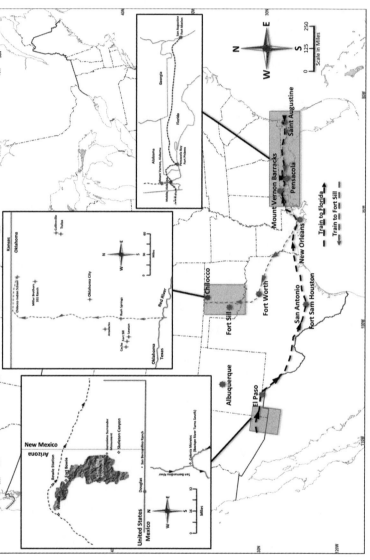

The odyssey of the Naiche-Geronimo band of Apaches from their surrender at Skeleton Canyon and train departure from Bowie Station in September 1886, six-week stop in San Antonio, and separation for the men to live at Fort Pickens and their families to live at Fort Marion until they were reunited in April 1887, while the rest of the Chiricahuas moved to Mount Vernon Barracks, Alabama. The Naiche-Geronimo band was also moved to Mount Vernon in May 1888 and lived at Mount Vernon for six years until finally all the Chiricahuas departed from Mount Vernon Barracks to Fort Sill, Oklahoma, in October 1894. W. MICHAEL FARMER

CONTENTS

Acknowledgments

I AM INDEBTED TO THE SUPPORT OF NUMEROUS DIVERSE CONTRIBUTORS to this work who range from archival librarians, to editors, to numerous historians whose traceable records have made this work possible, to friends who have opened their homes to me for work in the Southwest, all of whom deserve special mention. The patience, encouragement, and support of my wife, Carolyn, made this work possible. Erin Turner's support at TwoDot made this book possible, and her editorial judgments and suggestions have been impeccable. Melissa Starr helped with the textual edit. Lynda Sánchez has shared rare photographs from her collection developed over years of research with Eve Ball, and she has been a guiding light in understanding the Apache people. Most of the photographs in this work are from the National Archives and Library of Congress. Their work has given the public access to historical images that would not have been possible even twenty years ago. Meredith McDonough at the Alabama Department of Archives and History was helpful in securing a hard-to-find photograph.

Histories I found particularly helpful include those by Angie Debo; Robert Utley; Eve Ball, Nora Henn, and Lynda Sánchez; Alicia Delgadillo and Miriam Perrett; Lynda Sánchez; Sherry Robinson; Woodward B. Skinner; Edwin Sweeney; Henrietta Stockel; and John Turcheneske.

I especially owe a note of thanks to Pat and Mike Alexander in Las Cruces, New Mexico, who opened their home to me while I rambled through the surrounding countryside doing research, giving lectures, and signing books.

To the many readers of the original drafts of these essays, I owe my sincere appreciation for their support and comments.

Preface

Among the fiercest and deadliest Indians faced by Americans settlers in the last quarter of the nineteenth century were the Apaches, who killed nearly all they came across, destroyed property, and stole livestock and supplies for a living while trying to protect land they claimed as their territory. The great war leaders of the Apaches at that time included Mangas Coloradas, Cochise, Victorio, Nana, Juh, Chihuahua, and Loco, but at the final surrender, none were as well known or as feared by Mexicans and Americans alike as Geronimo. The Geronimo legend is a major thread in the tapestry of the American West. Yet the true story of Geronimo, an epic comparable to the great stories of the ancients such as *The Iliad* and *The Odyssey* of Homer, stands above the half-truths and distortions sleeping in book and movie myths.

Geronimo was not a chief, but a *di-yen*, a medicine man with supernatural power. In his wild and free days, Geronimo was a hard man, a killer with a merciless eye who destroyed any supposed enemy who crossed his path when he was at war. He drew pleasure from satisfying an unending thirst for revenge, killing all the Mexicans he could of any age or gender.

The true measure of a man comes not when he is in power but in how he handles himself when the boot of misfortune is pressed solidly against his neck to choke him. Geronimo surrendered for treaty terms that included promises that all memory of the bad things he and his followers had done would be wiped out (much of what they did was never forgotten), all the Chiricahua bands would be together and receive their own reservation with good water and grass for raising cattle (never happened), Geronimo's warriors would see their families within five days after their surrender (actually they waited at least seven months), and they would remain in exile in the East for about two years (the Chiricahuas were prisoners of war for twenty-seven years). Thus it was that Geronimo and the Chiricahuas became prisoners of lies. Geronimo was a prisoner of war for the last twenty-three years of his life, but he survived and prospered despite years that included many sorrows and trials.

This book contains true stories about Geronimo and the Chiricahuas during their years as prisoners of war. It is a collection of short essays and associated photographs or art designed to sketch Geronimo as the man he was in the time and society in which he lived—a complex individual filled with life and all its contradictions—forced to adapt to a society he had long disliked and didn't understand, whose members, he believed, had told many lies to acquire his surrender. All the essays are based on historical events published by creditable and respected historians using material recorded in memoirs, military records, newspaper accounts, reports to Congress, and oral stories told by event participants and astute observers.

Naiche, Geronimo's chief, gave a eulogy for Geronimo in Apache at a graveside service. The eulogy spoke of Geronimo's wartime accomplishments, his keeping of his word, promises made at his surrender, and his worst failure, which Naiche believed was his rejection of Christianity that he had accepted for three years. Naiche urged the assembled people to profit by Geronimo's example and not make the same mistake. In these true stories of Geronimo's life as a prisoner of war, I believe there are many profitable lessons. There is much to learn from the worst of times for this fierce warrior.

W. Michael Farmer
Smithfield, Virginia
February 2019

Prologue

Geronimo the Man

During Geronimo's twenty-three years as a prisoner of war, he escaped being hanged by civil authorities in Arizona, rose to national "superstar" status, and eventually became an astute businessman. He was invited to three world's fair expositions, as well as numerous parades and fairs in Oklahoma, and rode with five other famous old warriors in Theodore Roosevelt's 1905 inaugural parade. During his time in captivity, Geronimo became a justice of the peace at Mount Vernon Barracks and a village chief at Fort Sill, earning pay for his leadership under the rubric of army scout. At the 1898 Trans-Mississippi and International Exposition in Omaha, Geronimo publicly debated Gen. Nelson Miles about the lies Miles told the Apaches to get him and his warriors to surrender. During the debate, Geronimo, the Apache warrior, showed how Nelson Appleton Miles, the American general and commander of the army, had lacked integrity in his dealings with the Apaches. During his captivity, Geronimo fathered two children, lost three wives, and married two more. When he died of pneumonia after sleeping drunk all night in a cold rain, he left a small fortune in a Lawton, Oklahoma, bank, garnered from selling his autographs, autographed pictures, headdresses, bows and arrows, and other mementos. He was hated by some of his own people and loved by others, but respected by all.

It is easy to see from the oral history of those who knew Geronimo personally and from those who have synthesized his historical record from many pages of government reports and his autobiography that Geronimo was a man of many faces.[1-6]

1884 | 1890 | 1898 | 1908

Photographs of Geronimo during his years of captivity. Beginning in the top left corner and viewing left to right: Frank Randall photograph of Geronimo a year before his last breakout from Fort Apache; Silas Orlando Trippe photograph of Geronimo in 1890 at Mount Vernon Barracks, where he was a justice of the peace; F. A. Rinehart colored photograph of Geronimo in 1898, the year he attended the Omaha International Exposition; and A. B. Canaday photograph of Geronimo in 1908, the year before he died at Fort Sill, Oklahoma.

Geronimo was first and foremost an Apache. From the day he was off his *tsach* (cradleboard), he trained to survive and live off a hard land where one mistake could mean death, to fight expertly with all the weapons at his disposal—knives, bows and arrows, spears, war clubs, slings, and White Eye firearms—and to suffer long and stoically to win any battle. He lived in a matriarchal society where men became members of their wives' bands—if wealthy enough, they might have several wives—and did everything in their power to protect and preserve their families.[3] By the time Geronimo was about fourteen, he was looking after his widowed mother, providing her with supplies and meat for her cooking pot. By the time he was seventeen, Geronimo had taken his first wife, Alope, and they had three children in ten years of marriage.[4]

Apaches believed that if a person, even another Apache, was not family or lived outside the band (Geronimo was born a Bedonkohe Chiricahua Band Apache), then he or she was fair game for raiding or war. Apaches believed in the great creator god Ussen and that gifts of supernatural power might come to a person from Ussen to help his people. Apaches were phenomenal athletes who could easily run forty to seventy miles in a day, day after day. Their running skills made them look more like refugees from a marathon than Mr. World contestants. White Eyes like General Miles, directing soldiers fighting and chasing Apaches, quickly discovered that their men couldn't keep up with even Apache children in the rugged deserts and mountains of what is now the American Southwest and northern Mexico.

Geronimo was an Apache warrior. He came to the council of warriors when he was seventeen in the time of the greatest organizer and leader of the Apaches, Mangas Coloradas.[2] After the Santa Rita copper mine massacre of Mimbreño Apaches by James Johnson in 1837, Mangas Coloradas made unrelenting war against the Mexicans, who had owned the mine, and by 1838 it had closed, its supplies from Mexico and ore deliveries down into Mexico choked off by the Apaches.

Geronimo was an Apache war leader but never a chief.[2, 4] By about 1850, Geronimo, in his mid-twenties, was a major war leader for Mangas Coloradas. Geronimo and Victorio each led large groups (for Apaches) of fifty or more warriors raiding Mexican wagon trains, villages, and mines.

After Mexican soldiers near the town the Apaches knew as Kas-ki-yeh (probably Janos) massacred Geronimo's family and about twenty others, Mangas retreated back across the border and made ready for revenge the next year. When the Apaches returned to Mexico, they seemed to know where the commander and his soldiers, who had attacked their families in Kas-ki-yeh, were (Arispe, Sonora) and rode to face them head-on in a pitched battle that, because of his family loss, Geronimo was given to lead. At the end of the day, only a few Apaches, Geronimo among them, still stood on the field, but there were no Mexican soldiers left. It was the first time, but not the last, that Geronimo was the war leader in a great battle. He became recognized among his people for his tactical brilliance, and warriors readily followed him.[2, 4] During the years he led raids into Mexico, his thirst never slaked for vengeance against Mexicans for the murder of his first family.

Geronimo joined Cochise in raids and battles after Cochise went to war with Americans in 1861 for the "cut through the tent" affair with Lt. George N. Bascom. In 1872, after Cochise settled down on the reservation he wanted in the Chiricahua and Dragoon Mountains, he let Geronimo and his "brother-in-law" Juh occupy a part that had a side against the Mexican border, which allowed easy access for raiding into Mexico.

In 1876, two years after Cochise died, John Clum, agent at San Carlos, talked Cochise's sons Taza and Naiche into moving their people to San Carlos as part of the Bureau of Indian Affairs's consolidation policy. Two days later, Geronimo and Juh told Clum that they would return to their camp and bring in their people to go with the others to San Carlos, but instead they disappeared into Mexico.

Geronimo was paranoid. John Clum and his tribal police arrived at Ojo Caliente in late April 1877, surprised and captured Geronimo, and carried him and six or seven of his best warriors back to the San Carlos guardhouse in shackles in the expectation that they would be put on trial and hanged. Fortune freed Geronimo and the others from the guardhouse when the Tucson sheriff failed to take them into custody. However, those months in the guardhouse made him exceptionally suspicious (perhaps in many cases justifiably so) in his all his dealings with the Anglos and some Apaches. His paranoia drove him to three more reservation breakouts and to break his pledge to Gen. George Crook to return to Fort Bowie in early April 1886, which led to all the Chiricahuas being shipped to Florida after Crook resigned.

Geronimo was a devoted family man. A major reason for his surrender in September 1886 was his and his warriors' determination to be reunited with their wives and children. When Geronimo was finally reunited with his wives, Zi-yeh, She-gha, and Ih-tedda, and two children, Fenton and Lenna, at Fort Pickens in Florida, visitors reported seeing him holding his baby daughter Lenna in his arms and feeding her. Geronimo divorced his Mescalero wife, Ih-tedda, thus effectively freeing her and their little daughter Lenna from the prisoner of war camp. Soon after Ih-tedda and Lenna left for Mescalero, Zi-yeh, his only remaining wife, became pregnant and, in September 1889, presented him with another daughter, Eva. Sixteen years later, after her womanhood ceremony, Geronimo would not let Eva marry for fear childbirth might kill her as it nearly did his "sister" Ishton, wife of Juh, when she had his "nephew" Daklugie.

Geronimo was an astute businessman. After his surrender, he soon learned that there was money to be made from Anglos anxious to see the notorious figure who had killed so many of their fellows and had to be talked into surrender. At train stops, Geronimo sold buttons off his shirt and then sewed more back on to sell upon arrival at the next train stop. George Wratten, the Anglo interpreter and former chief of scouts who devoted his life to helping the Chiricahuas, helped him get photographs to sell to the gawkers and taught him to write his name for the photos and on paper for sale, and Geronimo made bows and arrows and Apache headdresses to sell to the tourists for a fine price. He got his autobiography published by dictating it, under strict rules of engagement, to an Anglo friend, superintendent of Lawton public schools S. M. Barrett, and taking half the profits, and he sold his artifacts at world expositions, local fairs, and parades.[4]

Geronimo was a *di-yen*, a medicine man. He believed he had supernatural power, and so did most Chiricahuas. He believed Ussen had given him his power and had told him that no bullet would kill him and that he would die in bed, and it was so.

Geronimo was a Christian—for a while. In 1902, missionaries encouraged him to study the teachings of Christianity but didn't let him join the church because he wanted to use it to increase his power. The next year, after being badly hurt from a fall off Zi-yeh's pony, Geronimo made a confession of faith the missionaries believed, so they baptized him and admitted him to the church. He led an exemplary life for about three years, but then decided the rules were too strict and returned to belief only in Ussen, gambling, and drinking. He was suspended from church membership in 1907.

Geronimo was Naiche's counselor. Supernatural power was needed to be a successful chief, but Naiche was not chief material when he was appointed chief of the Chokonen Apaches after his brother died of pneumonia in 1876. Four years later, living at San Carlos with his people, Naiche was wise enough to realize he needed help, asked Geronimo to be his counselor, and gave him his chief's power to make war. Although the whites were often confused about who was in charge, Geronimo was always deferential to his chief, Naiche.

THE BEGINNING OF THE END

Gen. George Crook, arguably the best Indian fighter in the army, had first come to the Department of Arizona in 1871 to bring the Apaches under control. He understood quickly that it would take an Apache to catch an Apache, and he created the Apache scouts. Within four years, Crook had most of the Apaches settled on reservations. He was then sent to fight the Sioux, Cheyenne, and Arapaho on the northern plains in March 1875.

As a result of inept army leadership managing the Apaches and the bungling bureaucrats of the Bureau of Indian Affairs, General Crook was sent back to command the Department of Arizona in September 1882. His objective was again to calm the Apaches on the reservations, who were being cheated and badly managed, and to stop the raids of those who had left the reservations for camps in the Sierra Madre.

Crook listened to the disgruntled reservation Apaches and made things right. Then, in one of the most daring army operations ever conducted, he took fifty mounted troopers and nearly two hundred Apache scouts on foot into Mexico and, in 1883, brought back over five hundred

C. S. Fly photograph of Geronimo discussing surrender terms with Gen. George Crook, March 1886.
COURTESY OF LIBRARY OF CONGRESS

Apaches, including Geronimo and Naiche's people, with little bloodshed, to resettle away from the heat and diseases at San Carlos for a much better life in the mountains around Fort Apache.

Two years later, a paranoid Geronimo, believing he was about to be arrested again, left the reservation and tricked Naiche and Chihuahua into following him. Within ten months, war leader Geronimo and other chiefs and leaders with him surrendered to General Crook in late March 1886 with the understanding that they would be exiled to Florida for two years before they were allowed to return to the reservation.

Two days later, Geronimo, told by a bootlegger he would be hanged when he crossed the border into Arizona, broke off with Naiche and eighteen warriors from the main band. Gen. Philip Sheridan, commander of the army and General Crook's boss, told Crook that with Geronimo's breakaway, the promise of two years' exile was no longer appropriate. Only unconditional surrender would be accepted.

General Crook, usually honest and forthright with the Apaches, didn't tell them of Sheridan's new terms. General Crook knew that if the Apaches had learned of the demand for unconditional surrender, they would scatter to the mountains and embroil the United States in an interminable war. Geronimo's group continued to raid and fight until late August of that year. Because of Geronimo's breakaway, General Crook was forced to resign as commander of the army in Arizona and was replaced by Gen. Nelson Miles.

This proved an unintended disaster for the Chiricahuas. The War Department and the Bureau of Indian Affairs had long wanted to move all the Chiricahuas off the Fort Apache reservation because of Geronimo's breakouts and the trouble that seemed to follow the Chiricahuas wherever they were on the reservation. General Crook had argued against removing all the Chiricahuas. He told General Sheridan that most of the Chiricahuas settling into reservation life after the Sierra Madre campaign in 1883 were peaceful and hardworking and that moving them could only cause trouble. Remembering southwestern blood and terror after forcing Victorio to leave the Ojo Caliente reservation, where he had wanted to stay, Sheridan agreed with Crook and left the Chiricahua at Fort Apache. However, General Miles proposed moving all the Chiricahuas east and holding them with the Geronimo band—once they were caught. He wanted to send the Chiricahuas to a reservation in the Comanche-Kiowa, Kiowa Apache country of southwestern Oklahoma, then part of the Indian Nations, but Congress had made it illegal to bring Indians from the Southwest to reservations in Oklahoma. Miles also thought the Chiricahua Apaches and the Kiowa Apaches, who were in league with the Comanches and Kiowas, had a familial relationship, when in fact they were often blood enemies and couldn't even understand each other's languages. With Crook out of the picture (Sheridan sent him to manage the Plains tribes overseen by the Department of the Platte), there was no one to oppose the foolish idea of moving the Chiricahua out of Arizona, and it went forward.

When the Chiricahua who didn't break away with Geronimo in late March 1886 returned to Fort Bowie, they were immediately sent east and kept as prisoners of war at Castillo de San Marcos (Fort Marion) in Saint

Augustine, Florida. After the Chiricahuas arrived in Florida, most of the children were taken from their parents and sent to the Carlisle Indian Industrial School in Carlisle, Pennsylvania. The educational objective at Carlisle, as school founder Capt. Richard Henry Pratt (later brigadier general promotable) said, was "to kill the Indian but save the man," as opposed to General Sheridan's comment (he claimed he never said it), "The only good Indians I ever saw were dead."

Part I

Surrender

After five months of pursuing Geronimo's band without any results, Gen. Nelson Miles was desperate and swallowed a little pride. He called on one of Gen. George Crook's officers, Lt. Charles Gatewood, whom he had replaced with his own man, who knew nothing about Apaches, and two scouts with relatives in the Naiche-Geronimo band to ride into Mexico, find Geronimo, and offer him terms of surrender.

The scouts, Kayihtah and Martine, along with Lieutenant Gatewood and interpreter George Wratten, showing exceptional courage against the possibility they would be captured, tortured, and killed, found and spoke with Geronimo and his little band of warriors. Two days later, the Naiche-Geronimo band agreed to surrender. By September 7, the band was on a train headed for Florida.

The surrender of the Naiche-Geronimo band resulted from a number of complex relationships between Geronimo and Naiche, Geronimo and his warriors, Geronimo and Lieutenant Gatewood and interpreter Wratten, and Geronimo and General Miles. Miles's failure to disclose the terms of surrender to his army bosses or the president meant that they would learn of them from Geronimo and Naiche. Part I, "Surrender," tells the stories of these relationships.

Geronimo's Relationship with Naiche

COCHISE HAD TWO SONS: TAZA AND NAICHE. COCHISE GROOMED TAZA, the elder son, to assume the leadership of the Chokonen Chiricahuas, even though the chiefdom of the tribe was not normally inherited. Cochise died in 1874. Taza became chief on Cochise's reservation, and Tom Jeffords, the man his father had agreed to with Gen. Otis "One Arm" Howard in 1872, remained his agent. Most of the tribe thought Taza would be a wise and good chief. However, about twelve warriors led by Skinya and his brother Poinsenay believed the older, more experienced Skinya should be chief and established their own camp in the mountains away from where most of the tribe lived. The argument over who should be chief came to a head on June 4, 1876, when there was a gunfight between the Taza and Skinya groups. During the fight, Naiche shot Skinya in the head and killed him; Taza wounded Poinsenay, and six others were killed. That ended the disagreement over who should be chief.[1]

On the day of the gunfight, John Clum, agent at the San Carlos reservation, arrived at the reservation to talk Taza and Naiche into leaving Cochise's reservation and moving their people to his agency at San Carlos. The move was part of the Bureau of Indian Affairs's poorly conceived policy of reservation consolidation. Taza and Naiche, honoring their father's dying wish for the Chokonens to avoid fighting with the White Eyes, agreed to settle at San Carlos.

Tom Jeffords told Clum that Geronimo, Juh, and Nolgee had a band living on another part of the reservation and were included in General Howard's original agreement with Cochise. Geronimo and Juh met with Clum four days later and said they would move too, but they had to go back and get their people. Clum agreed but sent a couple of his scouts

Naiche and Geronimo at the Nueces River resting with their band by the train carrying them east, September 1886.
COURTESY OF NATIONAL ARCHIVES

to shadow Geronimo and Juh to report if they were in fact moving to San Carlos when they returned to their camp. The scouts returned to tell Clum that Geronimo and the others had ordered the village dogs killed to keep the move silent and then taken their families and disappeared south across the border. It was the first time Geronimo had broken out of a reservation.

Clum was so full of himself for all his successful reservation consolidations that he decided to take a trip back east in September 1876 to show off twenty of the Apaches then at San Carlos, including chiefs

3

Taza and Eskiminzin. (Clum actually wanted an excuse to travel back east to marry a lady in Ohio to whom he was engaged. He put on the Indian show as a way to pay his travel expenses.) The tour ended in Washington and was a big success. However, while in Washington, Taza caught pneumonia and died. (Some Apaches believed Clum poisoned him, but that was clearly not the case. In fact, Clum gave Taza such a grand funeral that he had to borrow money for train tickets to get back to the reservation.)

The Chokonen Chiricahuas decided that Naiche, then nineteen years old, who liked fighting, drinking, and Indian dancing, should be chief. He was too young to be a leader, and even in his mature years, though a fine warrior, he lacked the temperament to exercise authority.[2]

A year after their escape, Geronimo and his people were captured in April 1877 by John Clum (the only time Geronimo didn't voluntarily surrender) at Victorio's Warm Springs Apache camp on the Ojo Caliente reservation in New Mexico. While there, Clum, following orders from Washington, talked Victorio into bringing his people to San Carlos, again as part of the consolidation policy that had brought Taza and Naiche and the Chokonens to San Carlos. Returning to San Carlos with Geronimo and six or seven of his leading warriors in chains, as well as Victorio, Clum put Geronimo and his warriors in the guardhouse and told the sheriff in Tucson to come collect Geronimo for civil prosecution for murder and horse theft, which meant certain hanging. The sheriff never came. Clum, in a bitter argument with the army over who controlled the San Carlos reservation, left in a huff, and, Lyman Hart, the new agent, seeing no reason to keep Geronimo in the guardhouse, released him.

In early September 1877, after three months at San Carlos, Victorio, outraged by Clum's false claims about what a heaven on earth San Carlos was, seeing his people starving and poorly clothed and dying of smallpox or ill with malaria, broke out with another Mimbreño chief, Loco, and 323 of their followers, leaving only about 20 people behind. Naiche and most of the Chiricahuas stayed on the reservation. Geronimo didn't leave either, and Hart made him "captain" of the Warm Springs people who had remained. Geronimo promised Hart he would not leave the reservation and would inform him of any talk from the others about a breakout. But dissatisfaction with life on the reservation continued to grow, and warriors began stealing guns and ammunition, and their women began putting aside food in preparation for a breakout. The breakout came on April 4, 1878, when Geronimo, Ponce, and other warriors left the reservation for Mexico. It was Geronimo's first San Carlos breakout. Naiche continued to stay peacefully on the reservation with his people.

In the months that followed, Victorio promised to settle on the Mescalero reservation. But after some bureaucratic gaffes over food supplies by an inept reservation agent, and believing civil authorities were about to arrest him, Victorio left the Mescalero reservation in late August 1879. He roared across the Southwest like a forest fire in dry tender, burning and killing nearly everything in his path. Armies on both sides of the border were desperate to stop him. Geronimo and Juh, knowing they might be implicated in Victorio's war and caught in the surround to wipe out Victorio, returned to San Carlos in December 1879 or early January 1880. Ten months later, Victorio, out of ammunition, was wiped out at Tres Castillos in Chihuahua. By contrast, Geronimo, Juh, and their followers had been living quietly on the reservation.

In July 1881, Nana, who had been Victorio's segundo, or number two, with about fifteen warriors, suddenly appeared out of southern New Mexico and began a raid lasting about six weeks that covered up to seventy miles in a day. He killed anyone in his path (about fifty people) and stole over two hundred head of horses and mules. The army sent eight companies of cavalry, eight companies of infantry, and two companies of scouts after Nana, but he disappeared south into the Sierra Madre, and the chase was abandoned.

Naiche, Geronimo, Juh, and their people on the reservation were not directly affected by Nana's raid, but the panic it instilled in government officials caused them to overreact to perceived threats that were not threats at all. The result drove once peaceable Apaches off the reservation and into camps in the Sierra Madre in Mexico, where they believed they were safe from bluecoat attack. On September 30, 1881, the peaceable Naiche and most of his Chiricahua warriors and their families joined Geronimo and Juh with their seventy-four warriors and headed south. This was the first known incident where Chief Naiche, then about twenty-four, followed Geronimo's lead off the reservation.

It is interesting to speculate that Geronimo and Juh's returning to San Carlos during Victorio's War, rather than joining Victorio or continuing to raid and make war on their own, was a primary reason Naiche decided to enlist Geronimo as his counselor and to give him the prerogative to make war. Naiche was in his prime, about twenty-three, and he had been chief of the Chokonen Apaches for about four years. In 1876, he had agreed with his brother Taza to move their people from Cochise's reservation to San Carlos, as John Clum had requested. Their guiding principle in this move was the promise they had made to their dying father, Cochise, to avoid conflict with the White Eyes whenever they could. Taza had died that year, and nineteen-year-old Naiche, who enjoyed fighting, dancing, and drinking and was unprepared to lead, became chief.

By 1880, Naiche had no doubt learned that he didn't have the temperament to be a chief, especially when it came to making war. He had no supernatural powers to help him, and due to the promise he had made Cochise, he didn't want to make war, despite his warriors calling on him to do so because living conditions were so bad.

Geronimo's voluntary return to San Carlos must have been a revelation for Naiche. Here was a *di-yen* with undisputed supernatural powers to help make war, and he was widely respected by many of his people as a war leader, one who was wise enough to avoid becoming entangled in a war that might be devastating to any Apache fighting the full power of the American army and of Mexico. The fact that Geronimo voluntarily avoided war with the White Eyes made him a natural choice as a counselor Naiche thought he could depend on. Additionally, with Geronimo's supernatural powers used in war, demonstrated ability to take the fight to the enemy, and wisdom to avoid war, Naiche must have concluded that, in addition to making Geronimo his counselor and medicine man, it would be wise to give him his power as chief for making war and make him war leader.

There followed nearly two years of peace after Geronimo and the other Chiricahuas returned to the reservation in early 1880. As Daklugie,

Geronimo's nephew, related to Eve Ball years later, Geronimo told him when they met at Fort Pickens after their surrenders in 1886,

> *I was never elected to chieftainship, I had this thing* [qualities of leadership] *also, and men knew it. Had Naiche been older, experienced in warfare, and a Medicine Man as I was, he would never have depended upon me to exercise many of his prerogatives. But he was not. And he was wise enough to know that the life of his people depended upon someone who could do these things. And I, rather than see my race perish from Mother Earth, cared little who was chief so long as I could direct the fighting and preserve even a few of our people.*[3]

In the years that followed, Naiche was content to let Geronimo take the lead in fighting and negotiating with the White Eyes. Naiche remained in the background during the 1883 surrender and the 1885 breakout, though in 1886 he formally surrendered to Gen. Nelson Miles along with Geronimo. However, in a number of cases Naiche exercised his authority as chief over Geronimo. For example, after Geronimo ordered the warriors to kill a child in a sheep camp taken in early 1882, Naiche ordered the child released unharmed.[4] After Martine and Kayihtah, scouts for Lt. Charles Gatewood came to Geronimo's camp above the big turn south by the Bavispe River and convinced Geronimo and the warriors to speak with Gatewood about surrender to General Miles, Naiche made a point of telling Martine and Kayihtah to tell Gatewood that he had Naiche's word that he would not be harmed if he came to the camp.[5]

After Naiche became a Christian, he encouraged Geronimo to become a Christian too, was delighted when he did, and was badly disappointed when Geronimo slipped back into his old ways of hard drinking and gambling on everything from horse racing to monte card games.[6]

However, when Geronimo held a big feast to celebrate his daughter Eva's coming-of-age ceremony, Naiche led the singing, while Geronimo led the dancing, and Naiche's village provided a nice spot of ground where the ceremony was held. When Naiche's children were sick, Geronimo used his power as a medicine man to help cure them. More than one who knew them said that they were friendly but not friends.[7]

Geronimo's Last Warriors

THE CHIRICAHUAS WHO HAD LEFT THE RESERVATION IN 1885, AMONG them the leaders Geronimo, Naiche, Chihuahua, and Nana, agreed to surrender to Gen. George Crook at Cañon de Los Embudos on the afternoon of March 27, 1886. Their expectation was two years of exile in Florida before they were returned to the Southwest. The next morning,

C. S. Fly photograph of Geronimo and warriors before surrendering to Gen. George Crook, March 1886. Naiche, on horseback, and Geronimo, standing, are at the center.
COURTESY OF NATIONAL ARCHIVES

Crook left for Fort Bowie to telegraph the surrender news to Gen. Philip Sheridan, commander of the army. Crook left Lt. Marion Maus in charge of the Apaches as they traveled north to Fort Bowie. On the morning of March 29, 1886, Lieutenant Maus learned that Geronimo and Naiche, with eighteen men, fourteen women, and six children, had left unseen and unheard in the night, taking only two horses and a mule from the Apache herd.

The band that had left the main body of Chiricahuas was made up mostly of family groups, and several members were in their teens or early twenties. Lieutenant Maus detailed an officer and some scouts to escort the main body of the Chiricahuas on to Fort Bowie, while he took the remaining scouts and followed the trail of Geronimo and the others into the mountains. Maus and his scouts, never seeing the fugitives and running short of supplies, soon had to return. Two warriors from the escaping band returned the next day and joined the group under the command of Lieutenant Maus. These warriors had heard people leaving in the night, thought something was wrong, and left with them. As soon as they learned the actual situation, they returned to the main body, leaving Geronimo and Naiche with sixteen warriors, which was the group that surrendered with Geronimo to Gen. Nelson Miles on September 4, 1886.

After their surrender, the warriors and their women and children were put on a train headed east with Geronimo and Naiche on September 7, 1886. After a stop of six weeks in San Antonio at Fort Sam Houston, where Gen. D. S. Stanley, commander of the army in the Department of Texas, recorded who they were, the warriors were then sent on to Fort Pickens on Santa Rosa Island in Pensacola Bay, but their wives and children were sent on to Fort Marion.

The following is a summary of the warriors who surrendered to General Miles, their ages, and their family relationships.[1, 2]

1. Geronimo, about sixty-three, and wife She-gha

2. Naiche, about thirty, and wife Hah-o-zinne

3. Perico, about forty-six (half-brother to Fun and second cousin to Geronimo but often called his "brother") and wife Bi-ya-neta

(stolen during the 1885 raid for wives when the Mescalero woman Ih-tedda was stolen and taken as a wife by Geronimo)

4. Fun, about twenty (half-brother to Perico and second cousin to Geronimo but often called his "brother"), and two wives, Tahtziltoey, with whom he had three children, and another whose name is not remembered but who is said to have been related to Jasper Kanseah, who was Geronimo's nephew and his youngest warrior.

5. Ahnandia, about twenty-six (second cousin to Geronimo but often called his "brother"), and wife Tah-das-te, who it is said Geronimo sometimes used as a messenger when he wanted to contact Mexicans or Anglos

6. Yahnozha, about twenty-one (brother-in-law to Geronimo and brother to She-gha), and wife Rachel Tsikahda

7. Chappo, about twenty-two (Geronimo's son by his second wife, Chee-hash-kish, and brother of Dohn-say), and wife Nohchon

8. Tissnolthtos, about twenty-six (Eugene Chihuahua's nephew), and two wives, Oskis-say, with whom he had five children, and another whose name is not remembered

9. Nah-bay, about forty-five, a wife (name unknown), and a two-year-old daughter

10. La-zi-yah, about forty-six (brother of Nah-bay) and wife (name unknown)

11. Beshe, about seventy, and wife U-go-hun (the parents of Naiche's youngest wife, Hah-o-zinne)

12. Moh-tsos, about thirty-seven, and wives Bashdelehi and Nahzit-zohn (Moh-tsos left Bashdelehi and Nahzitzohn at Fort Apache in the 1885 breakout and took another woman to Mexico. When the warriors at Fort Pickens were reunited with their families, Nahzit-zohn refused to go because Moh-tsos had left her at Fort Apache. It is relationships like that of Moh-tsos and his wives that kept the

army in constant confusion over who was married to whom and how many wives a man had.)

13. Kilthdigai, an unmarried warrior, age unknown

14. Zhonne, about thirty-one, unmarried (son of U-go-hun, half-brother of Naiche's wife Hah-o-zinne)

15. Hunlona, about thirty-one (nephew of Beshe, cousin of Hah-o-zinne) and wife Dolan, who was not with him at Fort Sam Houston

16. Kanseah, about fifteen, unmarried, and small enough to be called a boy by the whites at Fort Sam Houston (another example of why the army was rarely able to get an accurate count of warriors in a particular band)

17. Betzinez, about nineteen, unmarried (raised with Chappo "as though they were brothers," cousin to Geronimo)

18. Garditha, about ten, an orphan (not likely a warrior but included in the count as a boy at Fort Sam Houston).

The list of warriors with Geronimo taken at Fort Sam Houston shows it's a stretch of imagination to say that there were eighteen mature warriors in the band, one being a ten-year-old boy and another about fifteen, much more a novitiate age, but they were all fighters. It's also interesting to note that the army consistently underestimated the approximate ages of the older warriors such as Geronimo, sixty-three, who the army thought was about forty-seven, and Beshe, Hah-o-zinne's father, about seventy, who was thought to be about forty.

Lieutenant Charles B. Gatewood, the Bluecoat Geronimo Trusted

George Crook resigned as head of the Department of Arizona and was replaced by Gen. Nelson A. Miles. Miles was anxious to demonstrate he was superior to Crook as a general and in fighting Indians. He had fought the northern Plains tribes with some success but had never faced Apaches. Disputing Crook's strategy of using Apaches to catch Apaches, Miles decommissioned nearly all the Apache scouts.[1] Miles asked for and was given 66 percent more soldiers (a total of about five thousand) than Crook had thought he could use (about three thousand). In five months of operations, soldiers under Miles failed to capture or kill a single Geronimo warrior.

Miles, willing to do practically anything to prove he was a better commander than Crook, decided to swallow his pride and send an officer into Mexico to negotiate a peace settlement with Geronimo.

Lieutenant Charles Baehr (army records spell it Bare) Gatewood graduated twenty-third in his class of seventy-six in 1877. He was commissioned a second lieutenant in the Sixth US Cavalry, first served thirteen months at Fort Wingate, New Mexico, and then reported for duty at Camp Apache (two years later called Fort Apache). At Camp Apache, he became commander of the White Mountain Apache scouts from March 31, 1879, to June 30, 1880, and from November 12, 1881, until October 1885. Gatewood, from Virginia, realized his success and survival depended on understanding the Apaches and gaining their acceptance by listening to their stories and instruction in Apache-style fighting and living in a hard, rough land with little water. Gatewood gained their

First Lieutenant Charles B. Gatewood, commandant of Apache scouts, Fort Apache, ca. 1883.
The Apaches named him Bay-chen-dey-sen
(the one with a long nose).
COURTESY OF ARIZONA HISTORICAL SOCIETY

friendship and respect by never lying to them and always being just and doing the right thing regardless of the cost to his career as a commander.[2]

On July 13, 1886, General Miles called Gatewood to his office in Albuquerque. Miles ordered Gatewood to find the Naiche-Geronimo band and demand their surrender. Gatewood, who had serious health problems (articular rheumatism in knee, ankle, hip, and shoulder joints) and knew he could bear to suffer for only a limited time in the field, initially refused to accept the order. Miles increased the ante and told Gatewood he would make him his aide-de-camp when the mission was successfully completed. Gatewood considered his options and agreed to go. Miles had also asked two scouts to go, Kayihtah and Martine, because they had relatives in the Naiche-Geronimo band. (It's said he offered them a large monetary award to go, some say $50,000—they had no idea of the value, regardless of the sum—but they never saw a penny of that money and had to fight to get a tiny pension, years later, after being made prisoners of war.) Miles ordered Gatewood to use an escort of twenty-five mounted troopers so he wouldn't be kidnapped by the Apaches. Ultimately, Gatewood didn't use the troopers, knowing they would only slow him down and an expedition with peaceful intentions would not appear so if accompanied by twenty-five soldiers.[3]

After the meeting with Miles, Gatewood ran into George Wratten on a street in Albuquerque. Wratten spoke and understood Apache languages better than any other White Eye and had many Apache friends.[3] Gatewood, who had learned to speak Apache as a White Mountain Apache scout commander, recruited Wratten to go with him to be certain there were no misunderstandings of what was said. In late July 1886, Lieutenant Gatewood, with interpreter George Wratten, the two Chiricahua scouts, packer Frank Huston, three pack mules, and later courier "Old Tex" Whaley, a rancher, rode their mules into Mexico on one of the most daring missions of the Apache Wars.[4]

By the time Gatewood was well into Mexico, around August 3, his joints ached, he suffered from dysentery, and he had a bladder infection. He found Capt. Henry Lawton's command following Geronimo high in the Sierra Madre at the junction of the Yaqui and Aros Rivers about 250 miles south of the border. Lawton told Gatewood that he and his group could ride with him for protection, but if he, Lawton, found Geronimo, he would attack and kill him because he had orders from President Grover Cleveland. Eventually Gatewood separated from Lawton's command after following Geronimo's winding trail and then learning Mexicans at Arispe had contact with women from Geronimo who said he was interested in talking peace.

Following Geronimo's trail and running with a white rag held up on the end of a yucca stalk to show they were peaceful, Kayihtah and Martine found Geronimo's band on a flat-topped mountain near the great southward turn of the Bavispe River about thirty-five miles south of the border. They convinced Geronimo and the other warriors that Gatewood, whom they all knew was a just man who understood the Chiricahuas, had come to speak with them about peace and to offer terms from General Miles. Two days later, Geronimo and his warriors, accompanied by Gatewood and Captain Lawton, who had arrived nearby during Gatewood's talks but had not participated in them, headed north to a meeting with General Miles to surrender.

Along the way north, they passed first a Mexican command out to capture or kill Geronimo and next American army troopers who had scores they wanted to settle for friends who had been ambushed by the Apaches. The Apaches assumed Gatewood could get them past those dangers, and he did.

At Skeleton Canyon, where the surrender to General Miles was to take place, the increasingly nervous Chiricahuas had to wait six days for General Miles while Gatewood encouraged them to be patient. Lawton later said the sole reason the Apaches stayed in place together was because of Gatewood. In fact, in messages to Captain Lawton, General Miles twice subtly hinted that he would be happy if Geronimo and his people were killed trying to escape. Miles, hoisted on his own petard, was fearful that if he signed a peace agreement, Geronimo and others might break away again and cause him great embarrassment, like that suffered by General Crook when Geronimo decided to stay in Mexico.

General Miles finally appeared on the afternoon of September 3, 1886, explained terms to Geronimo, and then waited for Naiche, who was watching in the hills for a "lost warrior," to come in. The next morning, Gatewood and Geronimo rode to speak with Naiche and convinced him to receive terms from General Miles and to be part of the surrender ceremony that afternoon. On September 5, 1886, Geronimo, Naiche, and three others joined General Miles in his ambulance to return that day to Fort Bowie, sixty-five miles away.

Gatewood's return to the United States marked the end of his relationship with the Apaches. True to his word, Miles made Gatewood his aide-de-camp on September 14, 1886, and Gatewood naturally assumed he would then climb the military promotion ladder. He soon realized from all the political maneuvering within the army's Department of Arizona (General Miles was commander) that a scramble among the officers had begun for credit for ending the Geronimo War. For example, Lawton had written a report that praised the exceptional service of all officers in Mexico—except Gatewood.[5]

Gatewood's health had worsened since he had returned from Mexico. He applied for and was granted a month's leave of absence to recover but had to have an extension until he returned on March 22, 1887. While he was absent, the Department of Arizona moved to a small coastal suburb (Santa Monica) of Los Angeles. Upon his return, Gatewood saw that the infighting for credit for ending the Geronimo War had itself blossomed into a war, the victor claiming all the glory for the capture of Geronimo. General Miles's officers believed that they had tramped and sweated through Mexico and had therefore earned the victory. Miles made sure that they received their recognition. Recognition for Gatewood's contribution slowly dimmed and nearly disappeared. That summer, Arizona Territory announced that it would host a celebration to honor those who had ended the Apache threat. Expecting to be honored for his daring work, Gatewood ordered a new uniform for himself and a wardrobe for his wife. The celebration was to be held in Tucson beginning November 8. Just before time to leave for Arizona, Miles informed Gatewood that he would remain in Los Angeles to perform clerical work. So while all of Arizona cheered the military heroes—all except Gatewood—and Miles accepted an ornamental sword at the San Xavier Hotel for the capture of Geronimo, Gatewood performed tasks as an ordinary clerk in Santa Monica.

Gatewood had gotten in trouble with General Crook for insisting on justice for the Indians under his command, ending any chance for career advancement. General Miles and Gatewood clashed because Miles tried to charge the government for the use of household servants by calling them "packers." Gatewood was asked to sign papers stating that the household servants were packers. He refused. After Miles returned from Arizona, livid with rage, he ordered Gatewood to sign the papers. He again refused. Thereafter, Miles was after Gatewood's head, but Gatewood was careful and didn't fall for a Miles maneuver that could have gotten him a court-martial.[6]

As the years passed, Gatewood saw the ranks of officers who had been in Mexico in 1886 continue to rise, while he remained a first lieutenant and his health continue to decline. Even so, as a military officer, Gatewood was on the northern plains during the time of the Ghost Dance in 1890–1891, but he had no part in the killing of Sitting Bull or the Wounded Knee massacre. He was also part of the army command that had to deal with the Johnson County War in Wyoming between the cattle barons and the small operators and was badly injured trying to save Fort McKinney from a fire the small operators had started to drive the cattle barons out of protective custody.

Over the next few years, Gatewood's career continued to decline. In May 1895, he put in an application, endorsed by General Miles and others, for the Medal of Honor. However, in June the acting secretary of war refused to grant it since Gatewood had not distinguished himself in action. Putting his life on the line with honesty and integrity in dealing with the enemy didn't count. The verdict devastated him, and he made no further attempt to save his career. On May 11, 1896, not close physically to what he had been ten years earlier, he entered the post hospital at Fort Monroe, Virginia. On May 20, 1896, he died from a malignant tumor of the liver.

Gatewood was a man ahead of his time. The storehouse of information he gained from the Apaches in learning to be a good commander is similar to that of great twentieth-century Apache ethnologists such as Eve Ball, Morris Opler, and Grenville Goodwin, who, through years of hard work interviewing and documenting what their Apache friends told them, saved a cultural and historical tradition that could have been lost. The daily life knowledge Gatewood obtained and used to survive makes his views and observations invaluable in understanding the life of the Apaches.

The Decision to Surrender

IN LATE AUGUST 1886, GERONIMO'S BAND WAS CAMPED AND RESTING ON a flat-topped mountain at the bend of the Rio Bavispe around Sierra el Tigre, where the river turns near Colonia Morelos from running north to south. Kanseah, Geronimo's fifteen-year-old nephew, was watching the trail with field glasses when he saw two faraway scouts coming up the trail. He told this to Geronimo, who called a council and told the warriors that scouts were coming. Kanseah soon recognized them as Kayihtah and Martine and said they waved a white cloth, a sign of peaceful intentions. Geronimo said, "It doesn't matter who they are. If they come closer, they are to be shot." Yahnozha, one of Geronimo's best warriors, and Kayihtah were cousins. Yahnozha said, "They are our brothers. Let's find out why they come. They are brave men to risk this." Geronimo was angry that the scouts had betrayed them again to the bluecoats and said, "You shoot them!"

Yahnozha said, "We will not shoot. The first man who lifts his rifle I will kill." Fun, who by now was Geronimo's segundo, said, "And I will help you." Not wanting shooting between his warriors, Geronimo agreed. "Let them come." Yahnozha, jumped up on a rock and called to them, "Why are you coming?" Kayihtah yelled, "We come with a message from General Miles and Lieutenant Gatewood who want to discuss peace with Geronimo." Yahnozha motioned them to come in. They came to Geronimo and his warriors standing at the top of the trail. They greeted them and then led them back to their camp for a council. After the council rolled cigarettes in oak leaves and smoked to the four directions, Geronimo said, "Speak. We will listen."

Kayihtah said, "The Blue Coats are coming after you from the east, west, north and south. They've been told by their chiefs to kill every one

Chiricahua Apache prisoners (part of the Naiche-Geronimo band) at a rest stop beside the Southern Pacific Railway near Nueces River, Texas, September 10, 1886. Front row: L–R: Fun, Perico, Naiche, Geronimo, Chappo, and Garditha. Second row: L–R: Kanseah, Yahnozha; fourth from left, Ahnandia; extreme right, Beshe.
COURTESY OF NATIONAL ARCHIVES

of you even if it takes fifty years. Think on it. Everything is against you. If you're awake at night and a rock rolls down this mountain or a stick breaks, you'll be running. You even eat running. You have no friends anywhere in all the land. You're not at all like me. I get plenty to eat. I go wherever I want and talk to good people. I lie down to sleep whenever I want and get all my sleep. I have nobody to fear. I have my little patch of corn. I'm trying to do what the white people want me to do. There's no reason you people shouldn't do it. Don't you think my words are true?"[1,2]

Geronimo looked around the circle, and the all warriors seemed to nod their agreement with Kayihtah. Geronimo said to Martine, "You go to Gatewood and say, 'Geronimo wants to talk.' You come back with Gatewood. Kayihtah stays with us until you return."

Naiche said, "Tell Gatewood if he comes, I give my word he won't be harmed."

The next morning, Naiche sent three warriors with their weapons to meet Gatewood. They told him to leave any other soldiers and scouts except Martine and George Wratten, the interpreter, and come to a meeting at a bend in the Rio Bavispe, where, if trouble came, they could defend themselves and escape under cover. Gatewood, Wratten, and Martine went to the place on the river the warriors wanted, unsaddled their mules, and turned them out to graze on the good grass near the trees. The warriors joined them a few at a time, also turning their ponies out to graze; lastly, Geronimo came in. When he saw Gatewood, he laid down his rifle, and they shook hands. Gatewood passed around tobacco, and they rolled cigarettes in oak leaves to smoke to the four directions. This was serious business.

After they smoked, Geronimo said, "We come to hear General Miles's words. Give them to us!"

Gatewood replied, "These are the words of General Miles. Hear them. Surrender and you'll be sent to join the rest of your friends in Florida. There you'll wait until the president decides what he must do about you. Accept these terms or fight until you are all dead."

With the hint of a smile, Geronimo told Gatewood he had been drinking the whiskey they had been given from Fronteras after he had told the Mexicans he wanted to come in for talks. He said he felt shaky and, holding out his hands trembling, asked Gatewood if he had a little whiskey, but Gatewood told him he did not.

Geronimo steadied and put it to him straight. "I leave the warpath only if we can return to the reservation and live as before."

Gatewood shook his head. "General Miles's words won't change."

Geronimo then told Gatewood all the trouble they'd had at San Carlos and why they left. Gatewood was not impressed. He just sat and listened.

Geronimo and his warriors went off a little way and had their own council before eating a noon meal that Gatewood's packer provided.

After the meal, they gathered in council with Gatewood again. Geronimo looked Gatewood in the eye and said, "Take us to the reservation or fight."

Gatewood looked around to see if any guns were pointed at him, but none were. Naiche, who had been quiet during the council, held up his hand palm out and said, "Whether we continue war or not, you'll be allowed to leave in peace."

Gatewood nodded and said, "Hear me. You demand to go back to the reservation, but you have no reservation to return to. All your people have been sent to join Chihuahua in Florida."

Geronimo and the warriors were shaken at the news, but they returned to their private council place and decided to continue the war. Still, there were many things they didn't know about their families, who Gatewood mistakenly believed had already been sent to Florida. Naiche said they ought to kill a beef, stay in council through the night, and get as much information from Gatewood about their families as they could. They sent Kanseah out to find a beef, but none was to be had.

They continued to sit in council and smoke while Geronimo asked Gatewood what kind of man now fought him in place of Gen. George Crook. How old was he? How big? What were the colors of his hair and eyes? Was his voice hard or easy? Did he talk much or little? Did he mean more or less what he said? Did he have many friends among his own people? Did the soldiers and officers like him? Did he have experience with Indians? Would he keep his promises? The warriors listened intently to every answer Gatewood gave. After Gatewood answered all his questions, Geronimo said, "He must be a good man since the Great Father sent him from Washington, and he sent you all this distance to us."

As the sun was leaving the day behind the mountains, Gatewood said he and his men would go for the night to the camp of Capt. Henry Lawton, who had come up that day. This would give Geronimo and his warriors privacy so they could continue their own council, and to this they all agreed.

Geronimo believed Gatewood was an honest man with courage and respected him. As Gatewood was leaving, Geronimo said, "We want your advice. Consider yourself one of us and not a white man.

Remember all that has been said today, and as an Apache, what would you advise us to do?"

Gatewood thought for a little while before he said, "I would trust General Miles and take him at his word."

Geronimo looked around at his warriors and could tell they were thinking hard about what Gatewood had said. He told Gatewood he would tell him the result of their council when the sun brought the day again. He asked Gatewood to take one man and go to the nearest army post and, using the talking wire, ask Miles to change his terms, but Gatewood said the general had made up his mind. Geronimo believed Gatewood and didn't press his request any further.

The council lasted long into the night. After a while, quiet descended as each warrior decided what was best for him to do. Then Geronimo's brother (actually second cousin) Perico raised his eyes from the council fire, looked at each of the warriors, and said, "I'm going to surrender. My wife and children have been captured. I love them and want to be with them." Geronimo couldn't and wouldn't try to change Perico's mind, but he knew others would follow him. Fun said, "I'll surrender with my brother Perico. Our families are gone. There's nothing left here for us. We must return to them." Ahnandia, another "brother" of Geronimo and the husband of Tah-das-te, one of the women who carried Geronimo's messages to the White Eyes, said he, too, would surrender with Perico and Fun.

At first, Geronimo didn't know what to do. He thought for a while and then stood and spoke to them. "I don't know what to do. I've been depending heavily on you three men. You have been great fighters in battles. If you're going to surrender, there's no use my going on without you. I'll give up with you."

After the band decided to surrender, they determined how it should be done. They would travel with their arms to the American side of the border and surrender to General Miles if Captain Lawton would ride with them to protect them from Mexican and American troops. Gatewood would stay with them and, when convenient, sleep in their camp.

When they came to Captain Lawton's camp the next morning, they called for Gatewood and told him they would surrender and how they wanted it to happen. Captain Lawton and Lieutenant Gatewood agreed. Geronimo and his warriors moved their camp, including the women and children, down next to the army camp. Captain Lawton sent a rider to General Miles to tell him Geronimo's band had decided to surrender and that they would hand over their arms to him at Skeleton Canyon. Miles agreed to all of this.

The Apaches and Lawton's soldiers started north with Geronimo, Gatewood, Wratten, and the women and children in the lead, flankers on the sides, and Naiche and warriors in the rear to watch for attack. Captain Lawton's troop followed behind the Chiricahuas. On the third day, a big party of Mexican infantry soldiers, two hundred or more, came toward them from the direction of Fronteras. Lawton stopped to speak with them, while the Chiricahuas and Gatewood ran on ahead for an hour and then stopped and watched to see if there would be a fight between Captain Lawton and the Mexicans.

There was no fight. A rider came up to the Chiricahuas from Captain Lawton. He said the Mexican *commandante* demanded that Geronimo come and tell him personally that he had surrendered. Each side agreed to meet and bring only seven men. The American officers acted as neutral parties. Gatewood introduced the Mexican commandante to Geronimo. The commandante was quick to pull his revolver around to the front of his pants. Geronimo wasted no time pulling his revolver halfway out of its holster while staring at him with angry eyes, the whites of which seemed to turn red. The Mexican put his hands behind him, and Geronimo dropped his hand to his side.

The commandante wanted to know why Geronimo hadn't surrendered to him in Fronteras. Geronimo told him he didn't want to be murdered. Then the commandante asked if Geronimo was going to surrender to the Americans. Geronimo said he was because he could trust the Americans, and they would not murder him or his people. The commandante said he would go with the Chiricahuas to be sure they surrendered. Geronimo said, "No! I go north; you go south. I have nothing to do with you or your people."

The Americans asked Geronimo to let a Mexican soldier come with them to carry word back to the commandante that the Apaches had surrendered to General Miles, and he agreed to this. (After Geronimo formally surrendered, Miles sent the Mexican soldier back with a letter certifying as much.)

When the Chiricahuas reached Skeleton Canyon, General Miles was still fearful of meeting with them unless they were under guard. Captain Lawton became embroiled in a number of messages to Miles trying to convince him the surrender was the real thing. Geronimo sent Perico and Wratten to Fort Bowie in order to tell General Miles that the band wanted to surrender. Miles, with Perico and Wratten virtually prisoners at Fort Bowie, was still slow to make up his mind, and they had to wait a few days until he came.

Miles arrived late one afternoon. Geronimo rode down from the Chiricahua camp unarmed and shook hands with him. They talked and laughed a little, and then Miles stated his surrender terms. "Lay down your arms and come with me to Fort Bowie, and in five days, you'll see your families that are now in Florida with Chihuahua, and no harm will be done to you." He drew a line in the sand and said, "This line is the great water in the East." He put a small rock the size of a sling stone next to the line and said, "This represents the place where Chihuahua is with his band." He put another stone some distance back from the first one and the line and said, "This represents you, Geronimo." He put a third stone down, bigger than the other two and another distance from the rest. He said, "This represents the Indians at Fort Apache." Then picking up the last two stones, he put them together with the one representing Chihuahua and said, "That is what the President wants to do, get all of you together on your own good reservation with no one to bother you."[2, 3]

Geronimo smiled at Gatewood and said, "Good, you told the truth." Geronimo continued talks with Miles and told the general of the plot to arrest and hang him by Chatto and Mickey Free, army scouts, that made him leave the reservation, and Miles listened attentively. Geronimo said (probably as he had told General Crook, who said he lied),

I was living quietly and contented, doing and thinking of no harm, while at the Sierra Blancas (White Mountains). I don't know what harm I did to those three men, Chatto, Mickey Free, and Lieutenant

Davis [who was in charge of the Apaches at Fort Apache]. *I was living peaceably and satisfied when people began to speak bad of me. I should be glad to know who started those stories. I was living peaceably with my family, having plenty to eat, sleeping well, taking care of my people, and perfectly contented. . . . I hadn't killed horse or man, American or Indian. I don't know what was the matter with people in charge of us. They knew it to be so, and yet they said I was a bad man and the worst man there. . . . I didn't leave of my own accord. . . . Sometime before I left an Indian named Nodiskay had a talk with me. He said, "They're going to arrest you," but I paid no attention to him, knowing that I had done no wrong. Huera, the wife of Mangas, told me that they were going to seize me and put me and Mangas in the guardhouse, and I learned from the American and Apache soldiers [scouts], from Chatto and Mickey Free, that the Americans were going to arrest me and hang me, and so I left. . . . I want to know now who it was that ordered me to be arrested. I was praying to the light and to the darkness, to God and to the sun, to let me live quietly there with my family.*

I have several times asked for peace, but trouble has come with the agents and interpreters. I don't want what has passed to happen again. . . . Whenever I have broken out, it has been on account of bad talk. . . . Very often there are stories put in the newspapers that I am to be hanged. I don't want that any more. When a man tries to do right, such stories ought not to be put in the newspapers. There are very few of my men left now. They have done some bad things, but I want them all rubbed out and let us never speak of them again.[4]

Miles said he believed Geronimo. While they talked, Naiche waited in the hills to see what would happen. The next day, Gatewood and Geronimo went and brought Naiche in by telling him that Miles was waiting on him and that it was impolite to keep the general waiting. Naiche, a stickler for good manners, followed them in. Miles gave Naiche the same terms he gave Geronimo, and Naiche surrendered.

General Miles had a big surrender ceremony. He and Geronimo stood between his soldiers and Geronimo's warriors and placed a big stone on a blanket. For the Chiricahuas, this stone made their treaty. It was to last until the stone turned to dust. Miles and Geronimo raised their hands to heaven and took an oath not to do any wrong to each other or to scheme against each other.

Geronimo said that he promised to quit the warpath and live in peace forever. Miles smoothed out a bit of sandy soil and said, "Your past deeds shall be wiped out like this, and you will start a new life."[5]

Early on September 5, Geronimo, Naiche, and three other warriors joined General Miles in his ambulance and, under military escort, headed for Fort Bowie, sixty-five miles away. They made Fort Bowie in one day. Miles left Captain Lawton behind with soldiers to bring up the rest of the band, estimated to be a total of about forty. Lawton arrived on the morning of September 8 with the rest of Geronimo's band, including a new baby who had been born the evening before they started. Its mother was the wife of Geronimo's son, Chappo. While Geronimo, Naiche, and the other warriors who had returned with Miles waited for the rest of their band to arrive, they visited the mercantile stores and bought new boots and clothes for themselves, paying for the merchandise with money (depending on whose story you believe) provided by General Miles or from booty they had taken from Mexicans.

The day Lawton's contingent reached Fort Bowie, General Miles loaded them all on wagons and sent them as fast as possible to the train at Bowie Station. He knew that President Grover Cleveland wanted to turn the band over to civilian authorities for trials, which meant certain hanging for Geronimo and his warriors.

In a flurry of telegrams demanding to know why he had sent the Chiricahuas east, Miles never gave a direct answer about the terms of surrender. After three days, General Philip Sheridan ordered the prisoner of war train stopped in San Antonio until the army could get straight answers on the terms of surrender.

The Apache Prisoner of War
Train Stops in San Antonio

When the Chiricahuas were first shipped east to Florida, the train carrying the Naiche-Geronimo band was stopped in San Antonio. The Apaches waited nearly six weeks there at Fort Sam Houston while the Department of War and President Grover Cleveland tried to sort through General Miles's lies and distortions on the terms of surrender.[1]

Miles had known he was in a race against time to get Geronimo's band on a train to Florida before orders came from Washington directing him to turn the prisoners over to civilian authorities for trial and certain execution. In fact, the day before the rest of the band arrived at Fort Bowie (September 7), it was decided by the War Department that Miles was to hold Geronimo and the other warriors as "close prisoners" someplace in Arizona "subject to such trial and punishment as may be awarded them by the civil authorities of the Territories of Arizona and New Mexico. The women and children of his party should go to Fort Marion [Saint Augustine, Florida]."

It's easy to understand why the locals wanted to get their hands on Geronimo and the others after all the killing, robbing, and property destruction during their raids, but as Miles wrote his wife, the Apaches had "surrendered to brave men like brave men," and "we were honor bound not to give them up to a mob or a mockery of a justice where they could never receive an impartial trial." As soon as Capt. Henry Lawton arrived with the main party, Miles had them put in wagons headed for Bowie Station. Their train left Bowie Station at 2:55 p.m. that same day with Captain Lawton in charge of the guard detail.

Eugene K. Surtevant photograph of Geronimo on
Fort Sam Houston Quadrangle, San Antonio, 1886.
COURTESY OF NATIONAL ARCHIVES

As soon as the Naiche-Geronimo band headed east, Miles headed
north to check on the Chiricahuas who had peacefully stayed on the
reservation but were being sent to suffer in Florida all the same. The
Chiricahuas on the reservation had been tricked into all coming in to
agency headquarters to get rations and were arrested on September 5.
The women and children were sent back to their camp to collect a few
belongings while the men were kept under guard in a warehouse. Massai,

an army scout and the only Apache to escape the train heading east, tried to stir them up and break out, but the men had no weapons, and the army had their families. To try to escape would have been an exercise in futility, and they knew they could only lose.

On the morning of September 7, Lt. Col. James F. Wade had them loaded on wagons and taken to the station at Holbrook, ninety miles away. They reached Holbrook on September 12 and left the next day at noon. Most of the Apaches had never seen a train before, and some of the old ones prayed to it as it came steaming and whistling into the station. Terrified children ran off into the brush, but the soldiers soon found them and threw the women and children on board, and the men followed. They filled ten carloads. The windows had been fastened shut, and the only toilet facilities were buckets at each end of the cars. No one bothered to explain to the Apaches what the buckets were for, so many initially just used the train car floor for their natural needs. Even after the Apaches understood the purpose of the buckets, they often over-flowed, or their contents sloshed out onto the floor, requiring the trains to be hosed down. A carload of soldiers was on each end of the train, and four soldiers stood guard on the platforms between each car. It's easy to imagine how intense the heat must have been and how bad the stench as the train rolled across the deserts and plains in the late summer sun. The Apaches expected that they would be executed at any time and thought the soldiers, who laughingly used their fingers to make the cut sign across their throats, were friends trying to warm them of what was to come. On September 20, 381 Apaches (278 adults and 103 children) arrived in Saint Augustine, Florida, at Fort Marion. Chatto's group (ten men and three women), which had been sent to Washington to provide political cover for Miles and to beg that the scouts (some still enlisted) not be imprisoned, arrived at Fort Marion the same day. Geronimo's group didn't make it until four weeks later.

As soon as his superiors learned Miles had shipped Naiche and Geronimo's group east, they were on him. The questions burned up the telegraph: Why had he acted in "direct contravention" of Sheridan's September 7 order to hold them in close confinement at Fort Bowie until the president decided on their disposition? Miles gave a classic bureaucratic answer of ignorance: They were already gone before the order reached him. But the questions continued. Why the hurry to ship them without authority? Miles answered that he was still operating under March 30 orders, which were to place them beyond the reach of escape. There was no such place in Arizona. Therefore, he sent them to a more secure place of confinement.

On September 10, the War Department ordered Gen. D. S. Stanley, commanding the Department of Texas, to stop the Naiche-Geronimo train, take charge of the prisoners, and hold them until further orders. The train arrived with the prisoners on the same day Stanley received his orders. Accordingly, the prisoners were taken off the train and held under tight guard. The Apaches felt certain their execution was imminent, remembering the throat-slashing signs their "friends" the soldiers jokingly had given them earlier.

General Philip Sheridan and War Department staff began to realize that, despite what Miles had told them, Naiche and Geronimo "instead of being captured, surrendered, and that the surrender instead of being unconditional, was, contrary to expectations here, accompanied with conditions and promises." Again the telegraph hummed with the questions: What terms had been given them? Miles evaded a direct answer. General Stanley was directed to question the prisoners on September 29. In separate interviews with Naiche and Geronimo, with the post commander present, Stanley heard consistent stories. Both Naiche and Geronimo said they never thought of surrender until Gatewood and the two scouts came to them. They told of Miles promising to sweep away the past, his assurance they would be reunited with their families in five days, and his promise of a reservation.

After reporting the Naiche and Geronimo statements, General Stanley was directed to report on the individual prisoners and their characters and conduct. Stanley provided an account of each of the prisoners; he could not satisfy the order to state their characters and conduct since none would talk about the others, but he did say none caused any trouble.[2] Eight days later, President Cleveland directed that the prisoners be sent on to Florida, the warriors dropped off at Fort Pickens in

Pensacola Bay, and their women and children sent to Fort Marion in Saint Augustine.

The train carrying the prisoners left San Antonio on October 22. It arrived in Pensacola at 2:00 a.m. on October 25, 1886, with Naiche and Geronimo and their warriors; a train carrying their wives and children 360 miles farther east to Fort Marion arrived the same day.

The Last Apaches to Surrender in 1886

IT IS COMMONLY BELIEVED THAT THE NAICHE-GERONIMO BAND OF Chiricahua Apaches was the last to surrender, thus ending the Apache Wars on September 4, 1886. However, the last free Apaches to surrender were in fact the little band of Mangas, which surrendered to Capt. Charles L. Cooper in the mountains east of Fort Apache in the middle of October 1886.

Geronimo and Mangas had led the last breakout from San Carlos in 1885, and Naiche and Chihuahua joined them when Geronimo and Mangas told them that Lt. Britton Davis and Chatto had been killed and soldiers were coming to arrest the whole band and send them away. As soon as Naiche and Chihuahua discovered the deception, they threatened to kill Geronimo and Mangas, and the runaways broke up. This still left about 75 percent of the Chiricahuas living peacefully on the reservation. Mangas and his few followers left for Mexico and never rejoined the others. However, the bands under Naiche, Geronimo, and Chihuahua soon united with no evidence of bad feeling, and they, too, disappeared into Mexico, where their raids went unrecorded. As Angie Debo has noted, however, "There could be no peace on the American side of the border as long as they remained at large."[1]

According to the story Daklugie, one of the teenage boys with Mangas, told Eve Ball years later, Mangas attacked no one unless forced to do so in self-defense. Daklugie and Mangas's son Tsiltsoe (later named Frank at the Carlisle Indian Industrial School) were about a year apart in age. After the breakout, they acquired new revolvers and rifles and carried long spears and fine bows and arrows. Daklugie, who was about fifteen, carried a rifle and two revolvers and had about two hundred steel arrowheads that he had

Frank Randall photograph of Mangas, ca. 1884. Mangas was the last Apache chief to surrender. COURTESY OF LIBRARY OF CONGRESS

filed sharp and shaped so they couldn't be pulled out, which he carried in his quiver. If they were attacked at night, he and Tsiltsoe used their bows first, so they wouldn't give away their positions, and then finished up with their guns. Daklugie claimed he and Tsiltsoe could have killed many more Mexicans than they did, but in order to stay hidden and save ammunition, Mangas had forbidden killing more than they had to.[2]

Once they ran into Geronimo's group by accident, but they stayed together only a few days. Daklugie wanted to stay with Geronimo, but Mangas objected because he needed help protecting the women and children, and Geronimo supported Mangas in this decision. The bands soon separated, and Mangas turned north and headed for the border. They had lost most of their horses and mules and used the ones they had for pack animals. Because they were leaving the mountains, Mangas decided they would travel at night, which the Apaches didn't normally do, but it was much safer than daylight travel. He sent his son Tsiltsoe as a scout about a mile ahead and Daklugie about a mile behind. They would trade places when the moon reached the top of its arc across the night sky.

About 140 miles south of Deming, New Mexico, they discovered a herd of mules and were surprised that the animals weren't spooked by their scent. In fact, some of the mules looked familiar. They decided to take all of them so everyone in the little band had a ride, and the ones they didn't ride, they could use for food. Mangas did not approve of taking the mules, but he let them do it. He told Daklugie and Tsiltsoe the mules belonged to a big ranch, La Hacienda de Corralitos, that

Lieutenant Davis, having resigned from the army a few months before, now managed. (On October 9, 1886, Davis reported the theft of over fifty mules to General Miles and speculated they were taken by Mangas and his band, who, he believed, were heading for Arizona.)

With the mules in hand, Mangas headed for the border and Arizona as fast as the new mounts could take them. It was a long, hard ride, but they made it. Tsiltsoe and Daklugie took turns keeping guard when the band stopped to rest. For the next few days, they continued to wander north without being disturbed by the army. Like nearly all Mimbreños, Mangas desperately wanted to return to the land around Ojo Caliente in New Mexico, and he was heading there. Traveling at night, they followed ridges and made no fires, finally getting into the mountains east of Fort Apache before their luck ran out. Soldiers who had been fighting with some other band spotted Mangas's little group, which included two teenaged boys, two warriors, one named Fit-a-hat, an old and slow Mescalero, their wives, and three children. The soldiers attacked, but Mangas, Daklugie, and Fit-a-hat held them off until the rest of the band got away.

Mangas and his little band felt comfortably hidden until Tsiltsoe discovered a cavalry camp, which, according to Britton Davis in his book *The Truth about Geronimo*, was commanded by Captain Cooper of the Tenth Cavalry (nearly all Buffalo Soldiers) and consisted of twenty enlisted men and two scouts from Fort Apache. Tsiltsoe slipped close enough to the camp to determine that there was a scout with the soldiers. Daklugie and Tsiltsoe hated to tell this to Mangas because they knew it meant surrender. Mangas told Daklugie to scout the camp and, if the troops left, go in and talk with the scout who was acting as cook. He watched the camp for three days before he was able to enter and talk with the cook, who gave him coffee while they talked. Daklugie explained who Mangas's band was and asked the scout what they should do. The scout answered, "Give up. It's only thing you can do. Chihuahua has. All the rest have quit, except maybe old Nana. And he may have." (Nana had surrendered to Gen. George Crook with Chihuahua in late March of 1886 but then had hid out in the hills for a while because Crook said he didn't have to go to Florida). Daklugie asked, "Not Geronimo?" The scout said, "Yes, Geronimo. He and Naiche have already been shipped east on a train from Fort Bowie." The scout told Daklugie that they wouldn't be killed if they surrendered and that they would probably be shipped east with the rest. He advised him to arrange a meeting with Captain Cooper under a flag of truce and said it would be safe for Mangas to come in and talk with Cooper. And so it happened. Mangas walked in and surrendered. The scout told them that it was unbelievable they got as far as they did because the cavalry had been scouring the countryside looking for them. Daklugie said they probably were more interested in taking back the mules than they were in finding Mangas.[3]

After Mangas surrendered, the soldiers took everything Daklugie had, including his blanket, but they missed a long, thin knife he carried hidden in his long hair. He kept the knife through his days at Florida, Carlisle, and Fort Sill. Before the soldiers came to take Mangas's band in, Daklugie hid his war club in a hole he dug at the foot of a cliff. Years later, after he returned to live at Mescalero, Daklugie went to Fort Apache and recovered the club. He replaced the leather, and it was like new again. Before he passed away, he gave the club to Eve Ball out of respect for the work she had done in recording the stories the Apaches had told her and for helping them when they needed it.

From Fort Apache, the prisoners were taken to Holbrook by wagon to take a train east. The Apaches on the train endured the same horrific conditions suffered by Geronimo's band. The windows on the train car were fastened shut, toilet facilities were buckets on each end of the car, two guards were on the platforms on each end of the car, and a guard on the inside walked up and down the aisle. Every time the train stopped, the Apaches expected to be taken off and killed. Mangas tried to jump through a window but was only stunned when he hit the ground. He said he was certain the soldiers were going to violate his wife and didn't want to live if he couldn't defend her. Mangas was easily retaken and had his own personal guard in a seat next to him until he was delivered to Fort Pickens. The train left its warrior prisoners at Fort Pickens, as had been done with the Naiche-Geronimo band, and Daklugie was reunited for a few days with his Uncle Geronimo.

PART II

APACHE PRISONERS OF WAR IN FLORIDA AND CARLISLE, PENNSYLVANIA

All the Apaches taken prisoner of war and exiled were initially held in Florida at Fort Marion in Saint Augustine or Fort Pickens on Santa Rosa Island in Pensacola Bay. All but the Naiche-Geronimo and Mangas men were held at Fort Marion. It was impossibly crowded at Fort Marion, with over 480 men, women, and children crammed into a space its commander said was far overcrowded with 160 people. Food rations were drastically cut at the recommendation of the commissary general of subsistence, and the Apaches had to sell souvenirs and personal items to buy enough food to live. Children were separated from their parents and shipped to a school in Carlisle, Pennsylvania. The death rate for this once phenomenally healthy people soared to nearly three times the national average, and 25 percent of the Apaches died in the first three years of their captivity.

The children sent to Carlisle Indian Industrial School were intended to have their tribal culture and customs squeezed or beaten out of them as they were taught to read, write, do arithmetic, and learn a trade. This "education" was believed sufficient to allow the Indians to survive in the White Eye world and ultimately force an end to tribal life. Carlisle became an extension of Fort Marion for Apache children, who were also considered prisoners of war.

The separation of the Naiche-Geronimo and Mangas men from their families was a clear demonstration that Gen. Nelson A. Miles's promise that the Apaches would be reunited with their families within five days was another broken treaty term. There was plenty of room at Fort Pickens and virtually no disease. Eventually, the warriors were reunited with their families, and a year later, they were sent to join the rest of the Chiricahuas at Mount Vernon Barracks.

The little band of Mangas, son of Mangas Coloradas, surrendered about the time the Naiche-Geronimo band left San Antonio. Mangas, the young warrior Goso, and teenagers Tsiltsoe and Daklugie, Geronimo's nephew, were left at Fort Pickens, and their women and children were sent to Fort Marion. A few days later, Tsiltsoe and Daklugie were sent by train to Fort Marion to join those youths headed for Carlisle. By mid-1888, the Chiricahuas were out of Florida and living either in the piney woods surrounded by swamps at Mount Vernon Barracks or at school in Carlisle, Pennsylvania.

Life at Fort Marion, Saint Augustine, Florida

THE APACHES WENT TO FORT MARION IN SEVEN GROUPS. THE FIRST group comprised the nine hostages Geronimo had given Lt. Marion Maus as surety that he would show up for the March meeting with Gen. George Crook, which included Geronimo's Mescalero wife Ih-tedda and Nana and his wife, who was Geronimo's sister. The second group consisted of those who broke out with Geronimo and Naiche but surrendered in March 1886 and included the leaders Nana, Chihuahua, and Kutli. The third group had stayed on the reservation during Geronimo's third breakout and made up about 75 percent of the Chiricahuas, including the leaders Loco and Kaytennae (also a scout on the army payroll who went with the Chatto group sent to Washington first before being dumped at Fort Marion). Kaytennae had helped broker the first peace in March 1886. The fourth group consisted of the Chiricahua scouts who were still enlisted in the army and included warriors Martine and Kayihtah, who had helped talk Geronimo into surrendering on September 4, 1886. The fifth group, part of a doomed-to-fail face-saving political maneuver by General Miles, numbered thirteen and included Chatto, Kaytennae, other scouts, and three women. They had been sent to Washington to ask that the scouts be left at Fort Apache. When this group left Washington, they believed they were to return to Fort Apache. Less than a month later, they were staring at the nine- to twelve-foot-thick walls of Fort Marion in Saint Augustine, Florida. The sixth group included the women and children of the Naiche-Geronimo warriors who had surrendered in September. The seventh group included

Chiricahua prisoners of war not in the Naiche-Geronimo band were sent to Fort Marion (Castillo de San Marcus) in Saint Augustine, Florida. Over five hundred Apaches were kept there in terrifically overcrowded conditions. The sides of the inner parade ground are one hundred feet long. Approximately 150 prisoners had to sleep in thirty-eight tents on the terreplein top shown here. Others had to sleep in leaking casemates below, where the floors were always wet. There were only two bathtubs for the entire facility, and they were in constant use. The Apaches had to sell personal items to buy enough food to eat because they wouldn't eat fish, which they thought were unclean and unhealthy. The army reduced their rations for nearly two years. The death rate for the Apaches was three times the national average.
COURTESY OF NATIONAL PARK SERVICES

the women and children who had been with Mangas when he surrendered in mid-October 1886.

The Apaches were not the first Indian prisoners of war to be sent to Fort Marion. Warriors and chiefs from the Plains tribes had been sent there in the mid-1870s, and there Capt. Richard Henry Pratt got his start with his militarized Indian school approach carried on at Carlisle well into the twentieth century. Some of the Plains Indians had tuberculosis caught from white trappers, and it is believed that they left traces of it at Fort Marion and in Carlisle, where the Apaches developed the disease. Fort Pickens in Pensacola Bay had not housed Plains Indians, and Geronimo's people there didn't get sick from tuberculosis.

The first group sent to Fort Marion was shipped from Bowie Station, about eleven miles north of Fort Bowie. There were seventy-seven prisoners—fifteen men, thirty-three women, and twenty-nine children. Among these were two wives and three children of Geronimo and two wives, two children, and the mother of Naiche. They reached Fort Marion on April 13, one day after General Miles relieved General Crook due to his resignation when Geronimo failed to come in as he had agreed. Later that year, the War Department asked Fort Marion's commander, Lt. Col. Loomis L. Langdon (later to be commander at Fort Pickens), if he could take four or five hundred more prisoners. Langdon answered he could take at most another seventy-five, but he recommended not sending any more at all. He explained, in a revealing letter, the kinds of conditions under which his prisoners lived. Walls with casemates, once inhabited by the garrison, surrounded the small, one-hundred-square-foot parade ground. However, the terreplein above the casemates had become so dilapidated and leaked so badly that the casemates were uninhabitable. Langdon wrote that he had put up eighteen tents on the terreplein, which was fifteen yards wide with four-foot-high walls around the edges, to shelter the first group of prisoners and could possibly put up twenty more tents there to house eighty more, but, he said, sanitary conditions would be bad. There were only two bathtubs—one for men and one for women—in the entire fort. The fort was so close to and surrounded by Saint Augustine that it was impractical to put tents outside the walls or on some nearby islands, which overflowed with water in the winter. Nevertheless, Gen. Philip Sheridan passed Langdon's letter to the rest of the army command with a written comment: "The conditions stated by Col. Langdon need not interfere with sending the remainder of the Chiricahua and Warm Springs Indians to Fort Marion." By "remainder" Sheridan meant the nearly four hundred peaceable Apaches then living quietly at Fort Apache.

By the end of August, three of the young Apache children had died. One was the four-year-old daughter of Geronimo, who had been "feeble" when she arrived. Langdon and the post surgeon had tried to improve her health with milk and other good food to no avail. Langdon allowed the Apaches to go into town in small groups under escort to make purchases in the stores (often for food, which was in short supply by bureaucratic edict). The women did a good business in beadwork, and the men, in bows and arrows.[1]

On September 20, 381 Apaches arrived at Fort Marion from the reservation, along with the group of 13 led by Chatto who had been sent to Washington earlier; 70 were adult men, 221 were adult women, 41 were children between ages five and twelve, and 62 were children under the age of four. Fort Marion now housed over 450 Apaches when the commander had told the War Department it would be overcrowded with 160. Langdon put up as many tents as he could on the terreplein around the center drill area to house them. He allowed them to cook in leaking casemates with small fires as even wood was in short supply.[2]

Eighteen Apaches died at Fort Marion before the end of the year. The interpreters who had accompanied the Washington delegation, Sam Bowman and Concepcion, worked for a time at the post. Mickey Free, an army scout and interpreter who was not a Chiricahua, was sent back to Arizona. Langdon noted in his October 1 report that the Indian men, acting as sanitary police, kept the place "scrupulously clean" and that the two bathtubs (for 469 persons) were in continuous use. During September, Langdon reported seventy-six cases of illness, of which sixty seemed to be malarial ("intermittent fever"), and one old woman had died. The prisoners were to grow even more susceptible to illness when, after they had been receiving regular army rations, the War Department made a drastic reduction in food supplies on the recommendation of the commissary general of subsistence. Langdon protested that the amount was insufficient, but the regulations were issued on December 11, and rations were cut again on April 23, 1887.

Among the new arrivals were fourteen scouts whose enlistments had not expired. Rather than let them continue to draw pay, the army mustered them out, and they became prisoners like the rest on October 8. When the president and War Department began to feel the heat of public outrage at the unjust way the scouts had been treated, General Sheridan ordered Col. Romeyn B. Ayres, then commander at Fort Marion, to determine how many men had served as scouts. His report stated, "Of eighty-two adult male Indians confined at Fort Marion, sixty-five served the Government as scouts during the whole or a portion of the time Geronimo was out, that is from the Spring of 1885 until the Fall of 1886." Of the 365 women and children confined at Fort Marion, 284 made up the families of the scouts and of four subchiefs who were too old to scout but kept peace and order on the reservation.

During October, the Interior Department made plans to educate the children between twelve and twenty-two at Carlisle, and those younger were being considered. There were twenty-four boys and fifteen girls in the older group and forty boys and sixteen girls in the younger group. Angie Debo, in her book *Geronimo*, explains the numbers of boys and girls in the groups differed because a number of girls had early marriages, which precluded them from the count, and boy's ages were consistently underestimated.[3] In the older group, four were not well enough to go to Carlisle with the first contingent, which arrived there on November 4. Two days later, children in Mangas's band, including Daklugie and Tsiltsoe, arrived at Fort Marion. A second group of children, including others from Mangas's band, was sent to Carlisle on December 8. The total number at Carlisle from Fort Marion was then forty-four. Nearly half of these, including Geronimo's twenty-two-year-old son Chappo, became ill at Carlisle and were returned to their parents to die at the prison camps.

The Indian Office made a contract with the Bureau of Catholic Indian Missions for schooling the younger children on January 1, 1887. Before he was taken to Carlisle, James Kaywaykla, a boy who had ridden with Victorio and Nana, went to this school and later recalled, "I will never forget the kindness of those good women [the Catholic Sisters], nor the respect in which we held them. For the first time in my life, I saw the interior of a church and dimly sensed that the White Eyes, too, worshipped Ussen."[3]

The army moved the Fort Marion prisoners (except the families of Geronimo's warriors, who joined their men at Fort Pickens) to Mount Vernon Barracks, thirty miles north of Mobile, on April 27, 1887. They were held at Mount Vernon Barracks for over seven years before they were moved to Fort Sill.

First Days of Apache
Children at Carlisle

MANY OF THE YOUNGER CHIRICAHUAS WHO HAD BEEN INVOLVED IN THE
Geronimo surrender in 1886 and later came to Mescalero in 1913 encouraged the Mescaleros, through example, to rethink the value of White Eye
education and of living in good houses. These Chiricahuas were nearly all
educated at the Carlisle Indian Industrial School after being taken from
the prisoner of war camps at Fort Marion and Fort Pickens. Daklugie,
nephew of Geronimo, told Eve Ball the story of how Geronimo decided it
was imperative for his son Chappo and Daklugie to go this school to learn
the ways of the White Eyes and, more importantly, to escape being killed
when a new army command might decide to execute them. No such plans
existed, but Geronimo was always fearful of this. Daklugie and Tsiltsoe
were in their mid-teens and had been with Mangas's little band when he
surrendered in mid-October 1886. The train carrying the Mangas band
prisoners to Fort Marion stopped at Pensacola so that Mangas, a young
warrior named Goso, Tsiltsoe, and Daklugie could be held at Fort Pickens.

Daklugie was delighted to see his uncle and talk with him, until
Geronimo told him that he had the leadership qualities, more so than his
son Chappo, needed to lead the Chiricahuas and that, therefore, he had
to learn all the tricks of the White Eyes at their schools and stay alive by
going to a school. Daklugie was emphatic in telling Geronimo that he
was not leaving his warrior brothers to go to any White Eye school. He
would stay right where he was. Geronimo said (paraphrasing Daklugie),
"I'm the one who has the medicine here. You'll do as I say." So Daklugie
went to Carlisle.[1]

The first group of Chiricahua Apache children as they arrived at Carlisle from Fort Marion, Florida, on November 4, 1886. From left to right beginning in front row: Clement Seanilzay, Beatrice Kiahtel, Janette Pahgostatum, Margaret Y. Nadasthi-lah, Fred'k. Eskelsejah; second row: Humphrey Escharzay, Samson Noran, Basil Ekarden; third row: Hugh Chee, Bishop Eatennah, Ernest Hogee.
COURTESY OF LIBRARY OF CONGRESS

On November 1, 1879, army captain Richard Henry Pratt started the Carlisle Indian Industrial School to handle the training and education of Indians, many of them forced onto reservations in the 1870s. Pratt sincerely believed that Indians needed an American-European style education in order to take their rightful place in society and to be treated on an equal basis with the Anglos. For Pratt, that meant a student's Indian culture had to be destroyed on a student-by-student basis. To this end, Pratt's method was to take children away from their parents at five or six years of age, forbid the children, under threat of martial punishment, from speaking any of their parents' language or performing any custom or ceremony they had learned at home, require them to attend chapel every

Sunday and pray before going to bed and at rising, do everything according to command (a bell rings before students stand up or sit down, get in line, march, pick up a fork to eat, etc.), wear a uniform, cut their hair, and learn reading, writing, arithmetic, and some kind of trade (but never any preparation for college). By the time students were around eighteen, they would have had about twelve years of this schooling and would be allowed to return to their parents. By 1900, this was the way education was done at virtually every school for Indians, African Americans, Pacific Islanders, and Mormons run by federal or state governments in the United States.

Daklugie and Tsiltsoe were only at Fort Pickens a few days before the army decided that as teenagers who were not yet warriors, they should be sent to Fort Marion. When Daklugie and Ramona Chihuahua were small children, their fathers (Juh and Chihuahua) decided they should be married at the appropriate age, and they were promised to each other. Thus, when Daklugie arrived at Fort Marion, he was delighted to see his betrothed had survived and was also going to Carlisle. On the train to Carlisle, the girls sat at one end of the car, under the watchful eyes of an adult woman; the boys sat at the other end, supervised by a man. Their train became stuck in a snow-filled pass, and they had to wait three days before it could be freed. Daklugie always kept a small, sharp knife hidden twisted in one of his long hair braids. During a brief moment when they could speak with each other, Ramona asked Daklugie to kill her with his knife if White Eyes on the train attacked her, and he promised he would if he failed to defend her.

Pratt and three others met the train carrying the Chiricahua prisoner of war children at Harrisburg, Pennsylvania, and drove them by wagon to the school. The next day, the boys were all given haircuts and baths (Daklugie had taken his little knife out of his braid and hidden it in his blanket). They were all forced to give up their clothes and to dress in the school uniforms. After dressing, they were told to stand in a line with their backs against a wall. Daklugie went to the head of the line since (he said) that's where a chief belongs. Their interpreter then walked down the line and alphabetically named them. Daklugie, being first, was named Asa; then came Benjamin, Charles, Daniel, Eli, and Frank, which is how Tsiltsoe became known as Frank Mangas.

They were led to breakfast by their interpreter and seated at a table for eight (including the interpreter). The interpreter alternated the seating with a large boy, then a small one. The large boys were told they were to assist the small ones. Seated next to Daklugie was James Kaywaykla, the youngest Chiricahua at Carlisle. After they were seated, the interpreter told them the English words for tableware and food.

After breakfast, they were taught to make their beds and hang up their new clothes. Their old clothes were sent to their parents in Florida to prove their children were still alive. Each student was assigned household chores. Their interpreter advised them to do everything required, like it or not, and to do it cheerfully. Although such chores were irksome to the male Apaches, who had no desire to do a woman's work, they had been under a warrior's strict regimen for three years and thought this White Eye school business easy. They enjoyed the games and contests outside, the gymnasium, and playing in the band.

At first having to memorize everything because they couldn't read or write, they learned English, and before the winter was over, Daklugie was learning to read and write. He said his teacher was a very patient and kind white lady, not bossy as most white women were. One day she opened a big geography book and showed Daklugie Arizona. It was the first time in his life he had seen a map, and he was fascinated. She pointed out rivers and mountains, and he knew their names in Apache, some in Spanish, and a few in English. She let him take the book to his dormitory, where he and Frank Mangas nearly wore it out.

After Daklugie learned to read, he began reading whatever he wanted that was available in the school library. It was there he first learned from reading a newspaper that the Chiricahuas had been sent from Fort Marion to Mount Vernon Barracks near Mobile, Alabama, and that the women and children of Geronimo's band had been left at Fort Pickens with their husbands and fathers.

In the summers, Captain Pratt placed the Indian children in the homes of Dutch farmers in the surrounding area. They were given a small stipend (probably never more than five dollars per month) for their work. Daklugie's primary interest was in cattle. He believed raising cattle was as close as Apache men could come to hunting and fishing as a way of life and that they would never become farmers. Daklugie acquired every bit of information he could about cattle and their care and foresaw a time when his people would depend on them for survival. In a report to Carlisle, the farmer praised Daklugie for intelligence, reliability, and abstinence from drinking.

The Dutch housewives, who boasted their daily scrubbed floors were clean enough to eat from, taught the Chiricahua girls how to cook, clean, sew, care for chickens, plant and tend gardens, make butter, and can fruit.[2]

Student Life at Carlisle

Captain Pratt's method of educating Indian children was adopted by virtually every school in the United States educating other cultures and was driven by good intentions. The method was based on what Dr. C. L. Sonnichsen, great chronicler of southwestern history, called "determined ignorance."[1] Determined ignorance assumed, without any studied comparison, that Anglo society and beliefs were clearly superior to those of the Indians, that Indians were less moral, and that American-European Christianity was far superior to Indian religious beliefs, which were viewed as nothing more than superstition. The Chiricahua children sent to Carlisle were thus caught between two worldviews: those of their people and those of Anglo society.[2] If they survived at Carlisle, they were free to enter white society on their own. However, to the amazement of the Washington bureaucracy, nearly every Chiricahua returned to live with his or her people as a prisoner of war. Dr. Walter Reed, who showed that malaria and yellow fever were diseases carried by mosquitos, compiled statistics in July 1889 showing that of the 112 Chiricahua children sent to Carlisle, nearly a third, 27, died, 25 of them from tuberculosis.

The thing that made life bearable at Carlisle for the Chiricahua boys was athletic training. They enjoyed sports, and although the conditioning training was not nearly as difficult as what the Chiricahuas went through to become warriors, it was enough to keep them active and fit. During bad weather, they had access to the gym. All the Indian boys were good at wrestling; it was, in Daklugie's words, "a means of survival." On the other hand, he didn't think much of boxing. He couldn't remember men standing up to fight unless they had used knives. He said, "They were much quicker and more effective."

The same Chiricahua children at Carlisle School, March 1887 as those arriving four months earlier on November 4, 1886, and shown in previous photograph. From left to right beginning in the front row: Humphrey Escharzy, Beatrice Kiahtel, Janette Pahgostatun, Bishop Eatennah, Basil Ekarden; second row: Ernest Hogee, Margaret Y. Nadasthilah; third row: Samson Noran, Fred'k Eskelsejah, Clement Seanilzay, Hugh Chee.
COURTESY OF NATIONAL ARCHIVES

Track-and-field events, especially racing, were favorites among the Apache boys and men. One reason the Apaches liked track was that they wore running trunks and didn't have to wear long pants, which they hated. Daklugie and Frank Mangas specialized in "short" distances such as five miles. They considered long races to be marathons. The best marathoner at Carlisle at that time was a Hopi, Lewis Tewanema. He could start at an easy jog trot and keep it up all day. It was the kind of pace that would enable a man to outrun a horse over long distances. The

Carlisle marathoners often made training runs to Harrisburg (about twenty miles away) on Saturdays. Tewanema would suit up and play around in the gym for about thirty minutes, while the other runners took off for Harrisburg, unguarded because the Carlisle staff knew no runaway could get far in runner's trunks. After half an hour, Tewanema would start alone and then beat the others into Harrisburg. Returning to Carlisle, they all came back in the school's supply wagons. Tewanema was in the Olympic Games twice. He finished seventh in the marathon and second place in the ten-kilometer race.

In those days, Carlisle had one of the best football teams in the eastern United States. Its players were fast and husky, outrunning, outdodging, and outsmarting players on the other side. Pop Warner was their coach. He made star players out of boys who had never heard of football. Jim Thorpe, from the Sac and Fox tribe in Oklahoma, was Pop's best-known student. Gifted with natural athletic ability, Jim Thorpe was superior at almost all sports. Daklugie saw him play several times and liked to watch the games, but he thought football was silly and never played. He believed the only criterion for whether to play a game was if it helped teach him to survive. He said, "Leaving a place of ambush to knock your enemy down and sit on him was no way for a warrior to fight."

Carlisle students watched the football games from the stands. They wore uniforms, both boys and girls; the girls made theirs, and they were chaperoned by a female teacher. The boys and girls were not allowed to talk to each other, but Ramona and Daklugie managed silent greetings as they passed. Carlisle had a fine band that played at intervals during the game and paraded at half time. The band was so good that it marched in Theodore Roosevelt's inaugural parade in 1904. After football games, the students had parties in the gym, and some, to celebrate, did their native dances.

One Sunday morning at breakfast, Daklugie was told that Kanseah, the young warrior in training with Geronimo when Geronimo surrendered, was in the hospital. It was terrible shock. Daklugie knew that if students went into the hospital, they rarely came out alive. Daklugie obtained permission to visit Kanseah, who told him that he wasn't going to die and that he refused to swallow the medicine they gave him, spitting it out when the doctors and nurses weren't looking. Kanseah, probably sick from some form of pneumonia, did survive, but he was the exceptional case. Usually a student who became sick enough to warrant being in the hospital for any length of time was sent back to his family to die. Chappo, the quick, intelligent son Geronimo sent to Carlisle to learn the ways of the White Eyes and to escape possible execution if the army decided to wipe out the Chiricahuas, was sent back to Mount Vernon Barracks and died there on September 9, 1894, after six years at Carlisle and three weeks before the Chiricahuas were moved to Fort Sill.

At Carlisle, there were occasional misunderstandings between teachers and students that required cool heads on both sides. Daklugie told Eve Ball of an incident in which his teacher was having students use the dictionary to learn the meaning of words she gave them and write sentences using the words. One word was "work." The first definition for work that Daklugie found said it meant "ferment." He wrote, "I will not ferment in the house." The teacher became angry when she read it and told him to write a hundred sentences using it correctly. Daklugie said that he had used it correctly and wanted to know why she was punishing him. She made him go see Pratt, who made him wait an hour before seeing him. When Pratt asked Daklugie to come in his office, Pratt locked the door behind him, put the key in his pocket, and pulled out a blacksnake whip from behind a bookcase. Daklugie decided Pratt wasn't armed and took the whip away from him. Pratt grabbed him by the collar, but Daklugie grabbed Pratt's collar, lifted him off his feet, held him at arm's length, and shook him a few times before dropping him and saying, "If you think you can whip me, you are *muy loco* [very crazy]. Nobody has ever struck me in all my life, and nobody ever will. I could break your neck with my bare hands." Pratt stayed cool and politely asked Daklugie to sit down and asked why he disobeyed his teacher. When Daklugie explained, Pratt laughed. He asked him to go back to class and try to remember the many kindnesses his teacher had done for him. Pratt said, "You know that men must be courteous to the ladies and indulge them in their whims." Daklugie thought, *White Eyes! Their men spoil women. No wonder they are all henpecked. No wonder all white women are bossy.*[3] Daklugie went back to class and was never punished again. Despite his opinion that white women were spoiled, when he returned to Fort Sill he was angered to see Chiricahua women doing soldiers' laundry.

Daklugie, like many other students, considered running away from Carlisle more than once. But in Daklugie's case, he didn't want to leave Ramona and show up at Mount Vernon to face Geronimo and try to explain why he had left. Daklugie was at Carlisle for eight years and began to realize that some of the things Pratt required were beneficial and that Pratt's intentions for them were for their good, regardless of their dislike for them.

In the fall of 1894, the prisoners at Mount Vernon Barracks were sent to Fort Sill. This led to Carlisle sending its Chiricahua students back to their parents there. The girls went first, among them Ramona and Viola Massai. Viola married Ramona's brother, Eugene Chihuahua, who never went to Carlisle but learned to read, write, and do arithmetic while working for George Wratten, who ran the supply store for the Chiricahuas. When Daklugie was sent to Fort Sill, he saw how poor the Chiricahua cattle herd was. Captain Hugh Scott was in charge of the Chiricahuas. After a tussle with Captain Scott, reminiscent of the one with Captain Pratt, Daklugie was placed in charge of the herd. When most of the Chiricahuas moved to the Mescalero reservation seventeen years later, the herd was sold and was considered one of the best in Oklahoma.

Ramona and Daklugie were married in 1896 in two ceremonies, first as Apaches, as Daklugie desired, and then in a Christian ceremony, as Ramona desired. They lived a long and happy life together.

Apache Prisoner of War Life at
Fort Pickens, Pensacola, Florida

THE APACHES SENT TO FORT PICKENS ON SANTA ROSA ISLAND IN PENsacola Bay included those surrendering with Naiche and Geronimo on September 4, 1886, and, later, Mangas and Goso (Mangas's only mature warrior), who had surrendered on October 18. A train carrying the Naiche-Geronimo band prisoners left San Antonio on October 22 and arrived in Pensacola at 2:00 a.m. on October 25, 1886. After the men were taken off at Pensacola, the train continued on, carrying their wives and children to Fort Marion.

On the morning of October 25 at 8:30 a.m., a steamer pulled up to the dock where the fifteen prisoners waited and carried them on a short trip across the bay to a bright, white strip of sand with a few scattered bushes and scrub trees on rolling sand dunes—Santa Rosa Island. Less than two weeks later, Mangas, Goso, Daklugie, and Tsiltsoe arrived. Asa Daklugie and Tsiltsoe were sent on to Saint Augustine along with Geronimo's son Chappo; from there they were sent with a second group of children to the Carlisle Indian Industrial School.[1, 2]

On one end of Santa Rosa Island was a solid masonry brick structure, built around a hexagon-shaped center with two long casemate wings projecting in a shallow *V* off two sides separated by one panel of the hexagon. Fort Pickens had been vacant for twenty years. Lichens and mold discolored the bricks in the casemate, and it was overgrown with weeds, grass, and trees of good size. A pine tree even grew out of one of the chimneys. The commander of Fort Barrancas at Pensacola on the mainland, Lt. Col. Loomis Langdon, recently reassigned from oversight of

Fun, Naiche, Nah-bay, and Geronimo in the Fort Pickens casemates where they shared living space with thirteen other Apache prisoners of war, ca. 1887.
W. MICHAEL FARMER COLLECTION

Fort Marion, was also in charge of Fort Pickens. He put the prisoners to work for six hours a day, five days a week, cleaning up the place under the command of an officer and the interpreter for the Chiricahuas, George Wratten. The Apaches had leisure time on weekends except for washing and patching their clothes on Saturday. Two of the spacious casemates had fireplaces, and this is where the prisoners ate, slept, and spent leisure time. One prisoner was detailed as the cook using the fireplace. Langdon made sure they had plenty of clothing of the kind enlisted men wore for fatigues and enough blankets and bed sacks for their rough bunks, which they refreshed once a month with new straw.[3]

The officers in charge reported the prisoners were "neat and orderly in person, rooms, and cooking. . . . [N]ot once has the least sign of discontent or insubordination been shown." However, Langdon reported that in his opinion, they "really suffered at first owing to the smallness of the ration."[2] The Apaches were expected to supplement their ration by catching fish. Unfortunately, the bureaucrats didn't understand or accept that the Apaches wouldn't eat fish. Although General Sheridan was insensitive to the feelings of the Apaches, he refused to starve them and issued an order to provide them the food they needed. According to Langdon's January report, they were getting what they needed, even though their brothers and families at Fort Marion suffered from reduced rations for nearly a year.

The public, through the efforts of General Crook, soon learned of the indiscriminate punishment of the Apaches who had not broken out of the reservation in 1885. By March 1887, General Sheridan ordered an investigation into the treatment of the prisoners. The Indian Rights Association of Philadelphia, led by Herbert Welsh and Captain John Bourke, former executive officer for General Crook, inspected the conditions at Fort Marion in early March 1887.[3]

Welsh's report, published in April 1887, created a public uproar, and it began to dawn on President Grover Cleveland that peaceable Indians were being punished, that all were living under horrific conditions at Fort Marion, and that the prisoners at Fort Pickens had been separated from their families in violation of the conditions of their surrender. During March, the War Department considered sending all the Chiricahuas to Fort Pickens, which Langdon approved. Langdon suggested it be done in secret so that the railroad and other influential men would not petition the War Department to continue keeping them at Fort Marion as a big-time tourist draw. At the same time, tourists wanting to see the wild prisoners were also going in droves to Fort Pickens. Langdon required them to request a pass at Fort Barrancas so that he could ensure their reliability, but by the end of March, there were rarely fewer than 20 a day, and on one day, during a probable planned excursion, 457 people visited the island.

By mid-April, the War Department, feeling the public outrage from the Welsh report, decided to move the prisoners from Fort Marion to Mount Vernon Barracks thirty miles north of Mobile. On April 27, 1887, the train carrying the Fort Marion prisoners stopped in Pensacola. The families of the prisoners at Fort Pickens, numbering twenty-two women and eleven children, were taken off and carried to Santa Rosa Island by launches. The families of two or three of the men at Fort Pickens chose to go on to Mount Vernon Barracks, including Chappo's young wife, since Chappo was at Carlisle with Daklugie and others.

Geronimo was joined by his three wives: She-gha; Zi-yeh, with their six- or seven-year-old son, Fenton, whom Geronimo hadn't seen in nearly two years; and Ih-tedda (a young Mescalero woman he had kidnapped in 1885) with their baby daughter, Lenna, whom had he never seen. Naiche was reunited with his three wives, including one he had shot in the leg when she tried to run away to join the other prisoners the year before. Joining Mangas was his wife Dilth-cley-ih, the daughter of Victorio, and Huera, whom he had apparently divorced but with whom he didn't quarrel.

After family members sent to Fort Marion were reunited with the Fort Pickens prisoners, none died, except for Geronimo's wife She-gha. She-gha had been sick even before being put on the train to Fort Marion. It is generally believed she had pneumonia or perhaps tuberculosis, which she might have caught on the train or at Fort Marion. The general public, with their biases of superiority and thinking of the Apaches as savages, had no understanding of how glad the Fort Pickens prisoners were to be reunited with their families.

Langdon settled the families in casemates that had once been used as officer's quarters, so each family had an apartment of its own. The women did the household work, while the men worked outside, much as in white society and in accordance with Apache custom. Langdon commended them for their "cheerfulness of demeanor, for their prompt alacrity in obeying orders, and for the zeal and interest shown in the duties assigned to them."

As life assumed some normal stability at Fort Pickens, Geronimo, Naiche, and Mangas went to George Wratten and asked that he go to Langdon and tell him that "they were very desirous of going to permanent homes on land they could cultivate on their own." Langdon, unaware of the promises Miles had made them, told Wratten to tell them, "It might be remembered they had not as yet been punished for their crimes." Langdon thought that comment put an end to any thoughts about farms, but the Chiricahuas had Wratten write Gen. D. S. Stanley in San Antonio, asking him how much longer they would have to stay in prison and when would they get the good land Miles had promised them.

A year later, on May 13, 1888, the War Department moved the Fort Pickens prisoners to Mount Vernon Barracks. Except for the children at the Carlisle school, the Chiricahuas were at last reunited. It had been three years since Geronimo and the others had left the Fort Apache reservation where they had all been together.

Part III

Prisoners at Mount Vernon Barracks, Alabama

The Chiricahuas sent to Fort Marion in Saint Augustine, Florida, in 1886 were victims of severe overcrowding, short rations, and disease. (Despite Lt. Col. Loomis L. Langdon's protests, the commissary general of subsistence had recommended cuts in the Apache rations twice—on December 11, 1886, and April 23, 1887—forcing the people to sell personal items to buy food to keep from going hungry.) On April 28, 1887, the army shipped them to Mount Vernon Barracks, Alabama, about thirty miles north of Mobile, in the expectation that they would have much more room and a healthier place to live. The climate at Mount Vernon was actually worse than at Fort Marion. There were torrential rains, and mold grew on everything from food to moccasins. The people had to build little two-room cabins with dirt floors and cook over open fires in the middle of the room. The death rate from disease at Mount Vernon was about the same as it was at Fort Marion. Living got a little better and the death rate declined when the army restored them to full rations.

Apache Prisoner of War Life at Mount Vernon Barracks

THE NAICHE-GERONIMO BAND ARRIVED AT MOUNT VERNON IN MID-May 1888 from Fort Pickens about a year after the Chiricahuas from Fort Marion arrived. At Fort Pickens, the Naiche-Geronimo and Mangas bands had been short-rationed for about two months, while, inexplicably, those at Fort Marion had short rations for nearly a year. The members of the Naiche-Geronimo band at Fort Pickens were also much healthier than the ones at Fort Marion. In the nearly two years of

An Apache gathering at Mount Vernon Barracks, Alabama, ca. 1889.
COURTESY OF ALABAMA DEPARTMENT OF ARCHIVES AND HISTORY

captivity at Fort Pickens, the only death the Apaches suffered was that of She-gha, Geronimo's wife, who passed away at the end of September 1887. She had been ill from the time she had been sent east. In fact, the commander of Fort Pickens and others had recommended that all the Chiricahuas be kept at Fort Pickens, which was healthier and had much more room than Fort Marion, but army management was determined to settle them at Mount Vernon Barracks.

After Gen. George Crook's meeting with the Chiricahuas in early January 1890 and his subsequent evaluation and report, the army sent Lt. William Wallace Wotherspoon to take over as their special commander in June 1890. Wotherspoon was an efficient administrator. He soon established hospital facilities and let four men and their families live off base to work with local farmers for thirty-five cents a day. Recognizing that the cabins the Chiricahuas lived in were not much better than hovels, he picked a new village site on a ridge about three-quarters of mile from the main post. In 1891, Wotherspoon brought in a couple of carpenters who, along with George Wratten, taught the Apaches how to build snug, tight houses with wooden floors on firm foundations, finished inside and painted outside. They also learned how to furnish the houses with bedsteads and tables and chairs. Iron cooking stoves were provided. The women kept their houses neat and, being proud of their places, uniquely decorated them.

A year after Wotherspoon arrived, Secretary of War Redfield Proctor created an army unit, which the able-bodied men at Mount Vernon Barracks eagerly joined and, along with San Carlos and a few Carlisle students, formed Company I, 12th Infantry. This gave the Apache men work that earned them money for their families, taught them new skills, and allowed them to use war-fighting skills they had been developing since they were first off their *tsachs* (cradleboards).

During the time the Chiricahuas were prisoners at Mount Vernon Barracks, they did all they could to preserve their old lifeways. They gathered their children around campfires at night and repeated often-told stories of their history and traditions. They trained ceremonial dancers, carried on puberty ceremonies, and celebrated weddings as tribal customs dictated. For adolescent boys, they required a four-day fast and prayer ordeal to help get their vision in a quest for their medicine that would carry them through life.[1]

In early 1889, the War Department agreed to let the twelve Mescaleros who had inadvertently been made prisoners of war return to the Mescalero reservation in New Mexico. Ih-tedda and Lenna were Mescaleros and, therefore, free to return to the reservation. Geronimo divorced Ih-tedda to force her to leave him and return to the Mescalero reservation. His other wife, Zi-yeh, had a little girl eight months later. He named the child Eva, and it was clear to all who saw them that he dearly loved her. In 1893, a knowledgeable observer reported seeing him happily pulling Eva, then about three years old, in a little express wagon, accompanied by a smiling Zi-yeh, all clean and good-looking.

The same observer who described Geronimo pulling Eva in the wagon reported that the prisoners moved about the post and the reservation at will and were "daily met coming and going between their village and the trading stores." Although there were virtually no tourists in the area, the Apaches sold their crafts to passengers arriving on trains at Mount Vernon Station. Geronimo was a major player in this business and was described as having a sharp eye and being able to drive a hard bargain with his souvenirs, which included his signed photographs, war bonnets, bows and arrows, quivers, and canes. Wratten had taught him how to write his name, and for an additional fee, he would inscribe it on any of his merchandise. The observer noted, "He had a curious head dress, which he called, and Mr. Wratten says, was his war bonnet. . . . He seemed to value this bonnet highly, but finally, in his need or greed for money, offered it for sale for $25 [about $690 at today's prices]—his wife strongly objecting. . . . I finally bought it for a much less price, with a large bead necklace, which goes with it. . . . I asked him to write his name in the bonnet and offered him a pen for the purpose, but he declined the pen and went out and cut a small, dry twig, which he sharpened to a fine point, and then very slowly, and with much pains-taking, printed his name with the stick dipped in ink."[2]

The Chiricahuas tried to achieve a normal life in captivity. All their managers reported on their good conduct, their cheerfulness, and their industry. However, the women did gamble, and too many of the men had a strong taste for whiskey, which they could buy from bootleggers, white and black, just outside the military reservation fence. However, most of the time, sobriety was maintained by vigilant army officers and determined prosecution of the bootleggers.

Within a year after Wotherspoon became commander of the prisoners, he appointed Geronimo as a judge to try minor offenses at a monthly salary of $10.50. Not knowing at first what was expected of him in passing sentences, Geronimo was a hard judge. He sentenced one man to six months in the guardhouse for getting drunk and another to a hundred years in prison for being drunk and fighting. However, after he received some training, his penalties became much more reasonable.

At Mount Vernon, Chiricahua views on marriage and divorce began to change. In the more than seven years at Mount Vernon, there were only two known cases of marital infidelity. Corporal Fun, believing his wife Belle was having an affair, shot her and then killed himself. However, Belle soon recovered and went back to her parents. Another soldier also killed his wife and then himself. At the request of the participants, four marriages were made according to white customs. Except for marriages already in existence, polygamy had ceased among the Apaches by the time they left for Fort Sill in October 1894. After Geronimo, for example, sent Ih-tedda back to Mescalero, he never had more than one wife at a time.

Christianity grew in influence while the Apaches were at Mount Vernon. The post chaplain began conducting two services for them on Sunday—a Sunday school in the morning for the children and a service for adults in the afternoon. Both services were well attended. The "missionary teachers," for whose students Geronimo provided discipline, no doubt made religious instruction a normal part of their teaching day. Exposure to the Catholic nuns who provided the children scholastic instruction at Fort Marion must also have had an impact. Geronimo's wife Zi-yeh and his baby daughter Eva were baptized in the Catholic Church at Mount Vernon in July 1890.

As children grew to an age where they were ready for vocational training, Wotherspoon took the older boys out of their regular class after half a day of academic study to teach them carpentry while the village houses were being built. He recommended sending them to Carlisle or the Hampton Institute to learn a trade, but the War Department took no action. The Massachusetts Indian Association raised enough money to send four older girls to the Hampton Institute. The parents objected to the girls' being sent away, but Wotherspoon gave the well-known argument that the government knew what was best for the girls and not their parents, who would "sell them off to the highest bidder." The War Department agreed with Wotherspoon.

The army had an order that once students completed school at Carlisle, they were free to go and couldn't return to live as prisoners with their families. The order lapsed, and the students returned to their families. The bureaucrats had tried for ten years and failed to destroy tribal culture.

Geronimo's Wives

To the White Eyes, Apache married life customs were complicated. From pre-reservation days until after the turn of the last century, it was not unusual for polygamous marriages to exist among the Apaches. A warrior could have as many wives as he could support, and if he had more than one, the first wife was almost always designated the leader of the other wives. Apache society was matriarchal. Once a warrior married, he lived with his wife near her mother and father so he could help to support the entire family. This also meant the warrior became a member of his wife's band. For example, if a Bedonkohe Chiricahua warrior married a Mescalero first wife, then he became Mescalero. If a wife died, it was up to the family to provide a replacement (often a sister) if one was available; if not, the warrior continued to support the family for at least a year before he was free to look for another wife. If a husband died, then it was his brother's obligation to marry the widow. These customs, no doubt developed from long experience with what worked, were remarkably similar to the kinds of serial polygamy customs and laws followed by early biblical Hebrews.

Marriage customs varied somewhat from band to band. For example, nearly all Mescalero marriages involving more than one wife involved the marriage of sisters to a common husband. Avoidance customs, such as a man never seeing or being seen by his mother-in-law, among the Mescaleros were a major reason for serial polygamy with sisters. Wives from different families required separate lodges, which made a polygamous marriage very expensive, and avoidance of two or more different mothers-in-law made simple movement in a village unavoidably complicated. In other bands, the customs might make it much more feasible

Two of Geronimo's wives and their children. L–R, Ih-tedda with daughter Lenna on her right and son Robert Geronimo in her lap, ca. 1891; Zi-yeh and son Fenton ca. 1884; Zi-yeh's daughter Eva at about sixteen in 1905.[1]

PHOTOS OF ZI-YEH AND EVA COURTESY OF NATIONAL ARCHIVES; PHOTO OF IH-TEDDA COURTESY OF LYNDA SÁNCHEZ/EVE BALL COLLECTION

to have wives from two different families. In Apache culture, a warrior was so dependent on a wife's support for gathering and preserving food, maintaining the lodge and clothes, and guarding the village while he was gone, especially during wartime, that if he lost a wife and couldn't get her back, he kidnapped another woman and made her a wife, as Geronimo did with Ih-tedda.

One of the more confusing threads that runs through Geronimo's life is the question of who his wives and children were and what happened to them. For example, Angie Debo, in her biography *Geronimo*, says he had nine wives; another author, Alicia Delgadillo, in *From Fort Marion to Fort Sill* says he had ten; others have counted as many as twelve.[2–4]

In the beginning, Geronimo's first wife, children, and mother were killed by a Mexican army raid on an undefended camp around 1850, and Geronimo's life was changed forever. Thereafter Geronimo had at least two wives, often three, until after less than two years as a prisoner of war at Mount Vernon Barracks in Alabama, he never had more than one wife. The following is a list of his wives and a brief synopsis of their lives with Geronimo.

1. Alope, a Nednhi Chiricahua, a beautiful, slender girl, was Geronimo's first wife. They married around 1840 when he was seventeen and had just been admitted to the council of warriors. Geronimo, a Bedonkohe Chiricahua, had looked after his widowed mother since he was fourteen, and he had known and loved Alope since they were children. They were married for about ten years and had three small children before a Mexican Sonoran army raid into Chihuahua wiped out Alope, the children, and his mother. The old Apaches normally spaced their children about four years apart, which allowed the mother to maintain her work in food gathering and home maintenance for the family. This meant that the three children killed by the army were probably about nine, five, and one year old.

2. Chee-hash-kish, a Bedonkohe Chiricahua and, according to Betzinez, "a very handsome woman," was Geronimo's second wife. They probably married around 1852 or 1853. There is no record of Chee-hash-kish having children until she had a son, Chappo, around 1863 and then a daughter, Dohn-say, around 1866. For a wife to go ten or twelve years without having a child and then to have two within two or three years was highly unusual. Unsupported claims that seem beyond the bounds of normal Apache cultural life have been made that Chee-hash-kish had two more children during the early to mid-1860s who were older than Chappo and Dohn-say and whom Geronimo hid away in Mexico to continue his line. Chee-hash-kish was taken into slavery after being captured by Mexican troops at Rio San Miguel in 1882. Geronimo unsuccessfully tried to free her the next year by capturing some Mexican women, one with a baby, to trade for her release, but General Crook's campaign into the Sierra Madre in 1883 rescued the women and sent all the Apaches

back to San Carlos or Fort Apache. This left Geronimo with no one to barter for Chee-hash-kish and penned up on the reservation unable to do anything to free her.

3. Nana-tha-thtith, a Bedonkohe Chiricahua, married Geronimo soon after his marriage to Chee-hash-kish, leading to the first instance of him having more than one wife at a time. This suggests his rising importance since only a superior warrior could support two wives. Nana-tha-thtith had a child, but within two years of her marrying Geronimo, three companies of Mexican troops attacked the camp where Geronimo was recuperating from a wound while other warriors were off trading for blankets and supplies. Nana-tha-thtith and the child were killed. Even with one eye still swollen shut, Geronimo managed to put an arrow into a Mexican officer before escaping.

4. She-gha, a Nednhi Chiricahua and a close relative of the Cochise family, married Geronimo in the spring of 1861 after Lt. George N. Bascom had started the Cochise War. Her brother was Yahnozha, one of Geronimo's most dependable warriors. She-gha is thought to have had a daughter who died early. She-gha died as a prisoner of war after being reunited for a few months with Geronimo and two other wives at Fort Pickens on Santa Rosa Island. She-gha is buried at the Fort Barrancas cemetery in Pensacola.

5. Shtsha-she, a Bedonkohe Chiricahua, became the third wife in the family with Chee-hash-kish and She-gha. Shtsha-she was on the run with Zi-yeh and She-gha in late summer 1885 when they were all captured. Shtsha-she dropped out of sight at that time and no longer appears in any records.

6. Zi-yeh, also known as Taayzslath, a Nednhi Chiricahua, had a white father who had been captured as a young child and raised Apache.[5] He was a highly respected warrior named Jelikine (Pine Pitch House). Zi-yeh probably married Geronimo in late 1879 or early 1880. She had two children with him: a son, Fenton, and a daughter, Eva. She was a prisoner of war with Geronimo until she

died of tubular lupus at Fort Sill in 1904. She is buried at the Fort Sill Cemetery near Geronimo's grave.

7. Ih-tedda, a young Mescalero woman, was kidnapped by Geronimo's warriors in the fall of 1885 while she was gathering piñon nuts off the reservation with several other women. Geronimo had attempted to steal She-gha and Zi-yeh away from Fort Apache, where they were being held, but was only able to get She-gha and her three-year-old daughter. He needed an extra wife and claimed Ih-tedda. By the time Ih-tedda had joined Geronimo at Fort Pickens, she had birthed their daughter, Lenna. Geronimo, fearful of mass executions and disease in Alabama, sent Ih-tedda back to Mescalero with their child, effectively divorcing her. It was unknown to him that she was pregnant at the time. Soon after she arrived at Mescalero, her father married her off to an old scout, Old Cross Eyes, who collected a pension of eight dollars per month. Ih-tedda became Katie Cross Eyes and he, Old Boy. Katie registered her newborn son at Mescalero as Robert Cross Eyes. However, about fifteen years later, she changed it to Robert Geronimo. Robert and Lenna were Geronimo's only children known to survive to carry on his direct descent. After Geronimo sent Ih-tedda away, he never again had more than one wife.

8. Sousche (Mrs. Mary Loto) was a widow of about fifty-eight with a grown son. Geronimo married her on Christmas Day in 1905. He said they couldn't live happily together. She left him, which is the Apache way of divorce, in the spring of 1906 while he was still dictating his memoirs to S. M. Barrett.

9. Francesca was a great-aunt or grandmother of Eugene Chihuahua. Dates of this marriage are unknown. If the marriage occurred, it was probably at Fort Sill. Francesca had been captured in Mexico and held as a slave for about five years before she and others managed to escape. On the six-hundred-mile walk back home, she was attacked by a mountain lion, but she and the others fought it off. She was badly scarred and nearly scalped by the cat. No man wanted her for

a wife, but Geronimo, admiring her courage, is said to have taken her for a wife.[4]

10. Sunsetso or Old Lady Yellow, aka Azul, had been a Mexican captive as a child. She learned to speak excellent Spanish and escaped her captors. She had married but was a widow by 1906. She married Geronimo in 1907 and was his last known wife. They lived together at the home of Azul's niece's widowed husband, Guydelkon, in Perico's village at Fort Sill. Geronimo died in February 1909. His two-year marriage to Azul apparently was a happy one.

Geronimo, Mount Vernon Barracks Schoolmaster

THE CHIRICAHUAS SPENT SEVEN YEARS AS PRISONERS OF WAR AT MOUNT Vernon Barracks in the wetlands about thirty miles north of Mobile. In many ways, with a tip of the hat to Charles Dickens, it was the best of times and the worst of times, years when too many died, an epoch of forced idleness, a time when some men and women gained freedom, a time when new homes were built and new skills were gained, and there were days when understanding between the Anglos and the Apaches increased. One of those days of understanding came when Geronimo became a self-appointed schoolmaster.

About a year after most of the Chiricahua Apaches were moved from Fort Marion in Saint Augustine, Florida, to the Mount Vernon Barracks in Alabama, the Naiche-Geronimo band was moved there in mid-May 1888. The reunion between the two groups was a little slow to form because many of the reservation Chiricahuas, who had been unjustly imprisoned, blamed their imprisonment on Geronimo's staying out after he agreed to surrender to General Crook and spend two years in exile in Florida. The Chiricahuas had been moved to Mount Vernon Barracks in the beliefs that they would have more room, which they certainly got, and would be in a healthier environment, which they certainly were not. With the exception of building rough log cabins and growing small gardens, there was little to nothing the men could do to support their families. The soil was too sandy to grow major crops or support cattle, and most of the year the rains came frequently. This meant the adults spent most of their time playing cards or other games, and the children, nearly

Silas Orlando Trippe photograph of Geronimo at Mount
Vernon Barracks, ca. 1891.
COURTESY OF NATIONAL ARCHIVES

eighty in number, played and learned nothing educational that would support them in later life. The Apache leaders continued to ask about the reservation that they had been promised. By early 1889, General Crook and others had begun searching for a place the Chiricahuas could have as their own.

The story of the unproductive captivity of the Apaches in the early days became known through General Crook's newspaper interviews, and the resulting public outrage at the treatment of the Chiricahuas was a major factor in the army moving them to Mount Vernon Barracks. The Massachusetts Indian Association, a women's philanthropic society in Boston, sent two women, who had taught Indians at the Hampton Institute in Virginia, to gain an up-close-and-personal view of the Apache situation at Mount Vernon Barracks. They arrived in December 1887 with fourteen-year-old Parker West as their interpreter. Parker West was in the group of boys General Crook had sent to Carlisle in 1883 after bringing the Apaches back to San Carlos from their camps in the Sierra Madre.

The Massachusetts Indian Association's emissaries, free to walk through the camp and talk with the Chiricahuas as they pleased, found them to be

> *a keen and intelligent people. As we went about their camp they seemed to us a kindly, gentle folk, and their affection and confidence were not hard to win. . . . An intense love of their children is their most striking characteristic. . . . Our only obstacle came from fear that we had come to take more of their boys and girls from them. . . . The arguments and appeals that were made to us on this account made us glad that this was not our errand. . . . They kept letters and reports from Carlisle which were months old wrapped in pieces of cloth they had embroidered.*[1]

The visitors talked with the leading men about their hopes for the future. From this discussion, it was clear that the Apaches' first priority was to return to the land they loved, Arizona. However, understanding that white settlers were waiting for them to return in order to take their revenge against what they had suffered in the Apache Wars, the Chiricahuas were ready to remain in the East if they could have their own reservation. Nana was the only one who was not reconciled to staying in the East. Speaking in Apache, he was eloquent while he spoke a long time about returning to their homeland. Parker West, trying to convey the meaning of Nana's words, finally said with great emphasis, "He wants to know, 'Do you love your own HOME?'" One of the visitors showed

Nana a globe of the world and explained what it represented and that it was covered with people, so the Indians could no longer roam widely. This meant that they and the white men must live and work together like brothers. The women's report back to their society said, "The old chief sat with his head buried in his hands and said with a heavy sigh, 'I'm too old to learn that.'" In their report, the women also pointed out the need for a "missionary teacher" to carry out social and religious work among the prisoners, but they made no comment on government policy regarding their final settlement.[2]

The Massachusetts Indian Association raised the money and, with the War Department's permission, sent two teachers to Mount Vernon Barracks. Sophie and Sylvia Shepard arrived February 14, 1889. They or their successors continued their work for over five years, as long as the Apaches were at Mount Vernon Barracks. They taught about eighty children in a one-room building provided by the army for three years, and then an additional room was added in the fall of 1892. From the reports the army officers submitted to their management, the children "enjoyed the school and loved their teachers."

Geronimo had arrived at Mount Vernon Barracks about nine months before the teachers. He had seen seven or eight Chiricahuas die from diseases they normally never suffered, and he was still paranoid about the possibility of the army changing leadership and executing them all. During the time he had been a prisoner of war, Geronimo had decided that if his people were to survive as a people they had to learn what the White Eyes knew. Thus, Geronimo enthusiastically supported the new school. Appointing himself the schoolmaster, he brought the children into school and spent much time with them. He trained them with the same strict discipline he had used before his surrender when he trained boys to become warriors. He paced about the schoolroom with a stick in hand to intimidate any child who might be tempted to misbehave.[3]

General Oliver Otis Howard, who had agreed to terms with Cochise in establishing his reservation nearly eighteen years earlier, visited Mount Vernon Barracks in April 1889 to inspect the prisoners. Geronimo remembered meeting him in Cochise's stronghold and ran to throw his arms around him while excitedly speaking in Apache. After finding an interpreter, Geronimo told General Howard, "We have fine lady teachers. All the children go to their school. I make them. I want them to be white children."[2]

As time passed, the mild-mannered, dignified, and easygoing Chihuahua, whom the soldiers had nicknamed Chesterfield, was assigned to "maintain order" and work as a janitor. No doubt, it was a change welcomed by many of the students.

General Crook's 1890 Mount Vernon Barracks Visit

GENERAL CROOK'S VISIT WITH THE CHIRICAHUAS AT MOUNT VERNON Barracks, Alabama, in January 1890 was a turning point in the government's returning the Apaches back to the West and some ultimately to Mescalero, New Mexico, where their descendants live today. The Chiricahuas had great respect for Crook. When he first left the territory in March 1875 to fight the Plains Indians, he had established the Apache scouts, won the Tonto War, and maintained the Indians on

General George Crook and Geronimo ca. 1890.
COURTESY OF NATIONAL ARCHIVES

their reservations. He returned to Arizona in early September 1882 a year after Geronimo had left the reservation the second time, heard the Indian complaints about how badly the reservations were being run, again made sure the Indians were getting their due, and, in 1883, led a surprisingly bloodless campaign to bring the bands in Mexico back to the reservations.

After the Chiricahua became prisoners of war in 1886, General Crook, through newspaper interviews, fought tirelessly with the bureaucracy to rectify the injustice that had been done in imprisoning the scouts and other innocents, and he worked tirelessly searching for a reservation for the Chiricahuas in the East or in the Oklahoma Indian Territory. One morning in January 1890, Crook appeared unannounced at the Mount Vernon Barracks. Many of the Chiricahuas had last seen him in March 1886, when they had agreed to surrender and serve two years of exile in Florida. They were delighted at his visit and hoped he could help them get their lives back.

General Crook held a council with their leaders to understand how they managed as prisoners of war and to determine the best place for them outside their homeland in the Southwest. Geronimo, used to taking the lead in talks with the bluecoats, leaned forward to speak. Crook said to Wratten, "I don't want to hear anything from Geronimo. He's such a liar that I can't believe a word he says." When Wratten told Geronimo this, Geronimo crossed his arms, sat back, and listened. The other leaders didn't like Crook's treatment of Geronimo, but they let it pass as just bad manners. Crook addressed Naiche and asked why his band had broken away and why they killed people. Naiche answered, "Because we were afraid. It was war. Anybody who saw us would kill us, and we did the same thing. We had to if we wanted to live."[1]

General Crook then asked, "How did you come to surrender? Were you afraid of the troops?"

Naiche said, "We wanted to see our people."

"Did the troops force you to surrender?"

"We were not forced to do it. We talked under a flag of truce."

Wratten, who had been at the surrender, described how it had been accomplished. General Crook then asked, "Could the surrender have been made without the scouts?" Wratten shook his head and told Crook he didn't think so.[1]

The council told Crook of their pledge to keep the peace, how they had kept the peace despite their losses when they were taken from their farms and small businesses, and their ongoing hope for a better future. They told him how Gen. Nelson Miles had sent Chatto at the head of a delegation to Washington, DC, to ask Secretary of War William Crowninshield Endicott that the scouts and reservation Indians not be shipped to Florida. Chatto and the delegation were given a paper saying that they had been there, which they thought was a legal document allowing them to remain in Arizona, and a medal. The delegation was allowed to return as far as Fort Leavenworth before being stopped and redirected to Fort Marion with the other prisoners.

Chatto took the big silver medal given him in Washington off his coat and said to Crook, "Why did they give me this to wear in the guardhouse? I thought something good would come to me when they gave it to me, but I've been in confinement ever since I had it." He talked about how he had given up everything to make the Washington trip: He had fields planted in wheat and barley; he had a wagon where he made good money hauling hay and other supplies; he had thirty sheep that were increasing all the time, and he made money shearing them and selling the wool; and he had horses and mules that were worth a good deal of money. He didn't leave any of his property of his own accord. Chatto showed Crook figures that demonstrated the payment for his livestock was grossly inadequate.

Others told similar stories of property they had been forced to abandon on the reservation. The army had gathered up their livestock, sold it, and, with much accounting paperwork, doled the proceeds of the sale out to them in five-dollar-per-month increments, but all suffered losses. Noche said he had been paid for his horses but not for ninety cords of wood he had cut and piled up to sell.

Kaytennae told Crook he had lost his crop and his wagon. He reminded Crook of how he had gone to the March meeting when Geronimo first surrendered. He said, "I talked your talk to them and your mind to them. . . . I never did anything wrong and never went on the warpath since I saw you. I tried to think as you told me to and was very thankful to you, and very glad to see you again this morning, all the Indians were, even to the little children." Then he described his unproductive prison camp labor. "I help build roads, dig up roots, build houses, and do work all around here. Leaves fall off the trees and I help to sweep them up. I was working this morning when you came here. I don't know why I work here all the time for nothing. . . . I have children and relatives, lots of them, and I would like to work for them before I get too old to work. I'd like to have a farm . . . long enough to see the crops get ripe."

Chihuahua also said he'd like to have a farm and to support his family and that he had a daughter and two near relatives in school he'd like to see soon. He spoke of the wide, clear ranges of his homeland and the smothering forests of pines around him and said, "There are trees all about. I would like to go where I can see."

In the report he filed about his visit, Crook said simple justice demanded that those Indians who had served the government should not be held as prisoners, that new farms be given them, and that immediate steps should be taken to secure a reservation for them where they could support themselves and receive "the full benefit of their labors." He believed their high mortality was "due to homesickness, change of climate, the dreary monotony of empty lives."

Crook didn't recommend sending them back to Arizona. If trouble broke out and they went on the warpath, he said, "it would be utterly impossible to ever get them to surrender again." He said the cost in lives and property would be huge. However, he believed that, regardless of where they were placed, they would be as law-abiding as any community in the country would. He thought the best place for a reservation east of the Mississippi River was in North Carolina, but he preferred the Indian Territory, as it was more nearly like their homeland. He concluded that it was a mistake to send their children to Carlisle, which, for whatever reason, proved fatal to so many. He said, "Apaches are fond of their children and kinfolk, and they live in terror lest their children be taken from them and sent to a distant school."

Secretary of War Proctor immediately recommended to the president that the prisoners be settled in one of the two recommended locations with preference given to that in the Indian Territory. Politics got in the way of the government doing the right thing as recommended by General Crook in his report.[2] During the same session in which the president made his request for a Chiricahua reservation in Indian Territory, Congress was creating a Territory of Oklahoma and pushing plans to break up the reservations there for additional land openings. Four years later, after much political maneuvering, the Chiricahuas were sent to Fort Sill in Oklahoma, where they spent the next eighteen years.

Three months after meeting with the Chiricahuas at Mount Vernon Barracks, General Crook died from a heart attack on March 21, 1890. He was buried at Arlington National Cemetery. A reproduction of C. S. Fly's photograph of the meeting between Crook and Geronimo to discuss surrender terms in March 1886 was cast in his headstone.

Apache Prisoners of War
Become an Army Unit

KAYTENNAE, WHO BECAME A SCOUT AFTER GENERAL CROOK SENT HIM to Alcatraz for planning to murder Lt. Britton Davis, told Crook in their 1890 meeting that he and the other men wanted something to do with their lives for their families.[1] Secretary of War Proctor soon gave them the chance.

Most government officials held the theory that Indians should disappear as Indians and merge into the general population. Secretary Proctor's idea to accomplish this was to enlist them in the army, and he began with Apaches. In May 1891, Secretary Proctor created an Apache army infantry company, Company I, 12th Infantry, and invited able-bodied men at Mount Vernon to enlist. Forty-six enlisted in May, leaving only twenty-eight men in camp. Thirty-one men from other bands at San Carlos joined them, and a few students from Carlisle joined. It was the largest Indian troop unit in the army.[2, 3] The Apaches trained and did everything other soldiers did. By October, Company I was able to join the white units for drills and parades.

The enlistees were at once put to work building barracks, and they lived under the same conditions as enlisted men, receiving the same pay and subject to the same regulations. They drilled regularly and built bridges, learned maneuvers, learned White Eye scouting and tracking techniques (as if they didn't know better ones), skirmished in war games, which they enjoyed, and received an hour's instruction in English and mathematics every day. Additionally, there was training in blacksmithing and other crafts, and they played baseball and football. They became

Chiricahua members of Company I, 12th Infantry, ca 1895; back row: Toclanney, Tooisgah, Coonie, Tissnolththos, Mithlo, Yahnozha, Haozous; front row: Naiche, Mangas, Chatto, Kaytennae, Fatty, Perico.
COURTESY OF NATIONAL ARCHIVES

standard-issue soldiers with haircuts and uniforms and were even given names by which they were known thereafter. They also had their own noncommissioned officers, including Sgt. Burdett Tsisnah and Cpl. Larry Fun.

A better site for a new village on a sand hill about three-quarters of a mile from the post had been selected. With the War Department providing the materials, work had begun on the houses in early 1891 while the men were still prisoners, and it continued after they enlisted as soldiers. These houses were much better than the log-cabin hovels they had come to in 1887.

The only problem the Apache soldiers seemed to have was a weakness for alcohol, which, as Lieutenant Wotherspoon said, was "equal to—but not greater than—that of white soldiers."

The War Department considered the experiment of enlisting Indians in the military successful, but there remained much prejudice and resistance to using Indians as soldiers, especially Apaches. Additionally, everywhere Indians were enlisted, except at Mount Vernon Barracks, reenlistment was low. This meant that the days of Indian units in the army were numbered. By the summer of 1895, after the Apaches had been moved to Fort Sill, there were sixty-seven Apaches still enlisted there. Their commander, Capt. Hugh L. Scott, future army chief of staff, praised them for their drill excellence, guard detail reliability, and ability to maintain order in the Apache villages and to keep illegal Anglo cattlemen and traders off the reservation.

In May 1897, the Indian company held its last drill. Twelve of the Apaches were able to reenlist as scouts, but few of the others could find employment near the post, and they were soon starving. The army didn't help them or allow them to leave Fort Sill to find work. Many officers were still biased against the Apaches, despite their six years of excellent service. General Howard commented that men who detested the idea that they might have to take orders from Apache sergeants in the future resisted the idea of Apaches in the army.

The officers in charge of the Apache soldiers were uncertain what the status of the prisoner of war soldiers would be after their service had ended. Judge advocate Gen. G. Norman Lieber ruled that, because of their good conduct, all Apache soldiers would be free when discharged, regardless of their prisoner of war status when they enlisted. However, the army insisted that the freed soldier's families had to remain prisoners of war. All but two unattached young men stayed with their families.

Geronimo Counsels
Corporal Fun and His Wife

FUN AND PERICO WERE TWO OF GERONIMO'S MOST POWERFUL WAR-
riors, and he called them his "brothers" when he surrendered in 1886.
Actually, Fun and Perico were half-brothers and Geronimo's second
cousins. Fun was a hero among the Chiricahuas for being a fierce and
courageous warrior in the battle of Alisos Creek in 1882.

When Geronimo returned to San Carlos with a large cadre of warriors seven months after his breakout in September 1881, his supposed
objective was to save Loco's people from the misery of San Carlos. The
real objective was to get more warriors to help them fight the Mexicans.
Loco's people didn't want to be saved but were forced to go anyway.
Geronimo's warriors and Loco's people escaped from San Carlos and
made it across the border relatively unscathed. But at Alisos Creek, a
Mexican army detail surprised and attacked the escapees as they were
walking to a camp in the Sierra Madre. Fun, who was then about sixteen
years old, had a single-shot trapdoor rifle. By holding cartridges between
his fingers, he was able to load and shoot at a high rate of fire. He charged
shooting, zigzagging back and forth at Mexican soldiers, who repeatedly
attacked the Apaches taking cover behind the banks of dry Alisos Creek.
Because of this, he was given the Apache name Yahechul (smoke comes
out). More than one Apache witness to the fight said that Geronimo
stayed hidden with the women and children under the creek bank until
Fun had to tell him to get out and fight or he would kill him. Geronimo did get out and fight, and while the losses were heavy, most of the
Apaches got away during the night.

C. S. Fly photograph of Fun and Geronimo, March 1886.
COURTESY OF LIBRARY OF CONGRESS

When the army formed Company I of the 12th Infantry from Apache recruits, the best soldiers became noncommissioned officers. Among the Company I noncommissioned officers was Cpl. "Larry" Fun.[1,2]

About the time Company I was formed, Lieutenant Wotherspoon made Geronimo a "judge" or "justice of the peace" tasked with resolving internal Chiricahua disputes and misdemeanors under Anglo law. This soothed the old man's pride since the army thought he was too old to be a soldier, even if he was more fit than nearly all the white privates in the army. Geronimo did well as a justice of the peace, and his judgments were respected as wise and effective.

George Wratten, the official interpreter for the Chiricahuas, served as the superintendent for the twenty-eight men (including Geronimo) who had not enlisted in the army. Wratten had married Annie White, a seventeen-year-old Chiricahua orphan, in late 1888 or early 1889, and by March 1892 he was sensitive to the marital problems a young man his age could encounter.

Corporal Fun had two wives. His first wife, Tahtziltoey, gave him three children. His second wife was a beautiful young woman whose Apache name is unknown. She was related to Jasper Kanseah (a nephew of Geronimo and a warrior who had surrendered with him). Fun married his second wife about the time he joined the army.[3] Early in their marriage, he badly whipped her twice and had been strongly rebuked and warned about this behavior by Lieutenant Wotherspoon, his commanding officer. For several months thereafter, Fun and his young wife seemed to live in harmony. In early 1892, Fun began to suspect his wife of having "undue intimacy with two men." Rather than beat her again, he reported his suspicions to Lieutenant Wotherspoon, who had the charges fully investigated and became convinced Fun's wife was not having any affairs. When he told Fun the results of his investigation, Fun seemed satisfied, and there was another reconciliation.

On March 7, 1892, George Wratten noticed that Fun had returned to his belief that his wife might be unfaithful. Wratten called the couple into his office. After they talked and the couple left, Wratten was not satisfied about the situation. He asked Geronimo, as judge for the village and Fun's wartime leader, to act as their counselor.

Geronimo agreed to serve as a counselor and talked to the couple for about two hours that night. Fun appeared to be satisfied when he left, but Geronimo had his doubts. Geronimo reported to Wratten that "there was nothing wrong with the wife, it was all in Fun's brain." As events would soon show, Geronimo had sized up the situation correctly.[1]

The next day Fun was corporal of the guard at the Chiricahua village. Later in the day, he attended lectures and watched his men at target practice before returning to the company guardhouse. He kept watching his house as he sat in the guardhouse doorway cleaning his rifle. Shortly after dark, he went to his house carrying his rifle. He found his wife sitting on the floor and, without saying a word, shot her. The bullet passed down the fleshy part of her shoulder and was only a flesh wound. An old woman passing by tried to take the rifle away from him, but Fun, threatening to shoot her, drove her away. Believing he had killed his wife and would suffer the shame of being hanged, Fun put the rifle near his head and pulled the trigger, but the shot barely grazed him. He then put the end of the barrel under an ear and blew his brains out.[1, 2]

The shooting caused a major stir in the village with threats of revenge against Fun's wife because many believed it was her fault that he had killed himself. Many of the Apaches showed great presence of mind by hiding knives, axes, and other items that could be used as weapons. Within minutes, soldiers and officers were on the scene calming the situation, and within a couple of hours, all was quiet. The post doctor treated the wound Fun's wife suffered, and within a few weeks, she returned to her parents to live a normal life. Since Fun was on active duty, he was buried with full military honors at the Mobile National Cemetery.[3]

Fun's suicide was extraordinary for at least two reasons. First, suicide among the Apaches was extremely rare and normally occurred as a last resort during war. For example, it's claimed that, when he ran out of bullets fighting the Mexican army at Tres Castillos, Victorio stabbed himself in the heart. Second, Apache women were among the chastest of all the tribes, and charges of adultery were extremely rare. In fact, in nearly eight years, the Apaches (over 340 of them) suffered only one other suicide besides that of Corporal Fun, and both cases involved charges of adultery later learned to be unfounded.[2]

The Apaches March
to Mobile and Back

At the peak of its enlistment, Company I had seventy-six Apaches from different bands. At that time, there were three white sergeants and four Apache corporals (three Chiricahua prisoners of war and one from San Carlos). Some Apaches served briefly as noncommissioned officers but didn't like the responsibility and asked to be demoted. For example, Naiche, hereditary Chiricahua chief, served as a corporal for a while and then asked to step down. Mangas, a Mimbreño chief, refused to take a leadership role and remained a private.

By 1892, the Department of Missouri army units were taking one-hundred-mile marches as part of a fitness program. Lieutenant Wotherspoon, very proud of the progress of Company I, made a request on March 7, 1892, to Gen. John McAllister Schofield, commanding general of the army, that the company be allowed to do a ten-day practice march to Mobile with an extended stay over the weekend. Wotherspoon was anxious to show Secretary of War Proctor, the Indian Rights Association, other army officers, and people in the West that the Apache company was just as trustworthy and friendly as any other military unit in the army. Corporal Fun's tragic suicide occurred on March 8, but Wotherspoon didn't immediately report it. Fun's attempted murder of his wife and his subsequent suicide could easily have caused cancellation of the march had the Apaches not showed discipline and restraint in how they dealt with it. General Schofield wired his approval for the training march on March 9.

When there were no repercussions and no Mobile protests, the Apache column left the Chiricahua village at a little after 8:00 a.m.

Company I, 12th Infantry after marching thirty-eight miles in six hours and twenty minutes, ca. 1892.
COURTESY OF NATIONAL ARCHIVES

on Friday, March 11. The column had three white officers, three white sergeants, four Apache corporals, two Apache musicians (buglers), and sixty-five Apache privates. Tents and rations were loaded onto a large covered wagon drawn by a four-mule team. The men marched with bedding, canteens, haversacks, field belts, entrenching tools, and rifles. They were fully equipped as if they were taking to the field in time of war, except their bullets were blanks. They had also just been paid, and the Apaches had over $2,000 among them. The wagon driven by a soldier on loan from the quartermaster at the Mount Vernon garrison followed the wagon road that ran close to the Mobile and Birmingham Railroad tracks. The soldiers zigzagged through woods and swamps back and forth across the tracks. They camped the first night at Gunnison's Creek, where tents were pitched and guards mounted by 4:30 p.m. They had covered seventeen and a half miles.[1]

On the second day, Saturday, March 12, 1892, reveille was blown at 5:00 a.m., and by 6:35 a.m. the company was crossing the Gunnison's

Creek Bridge. They made such good time that Wotherspoon zigzagged again three times across railroad tracks and had them pass through several swamps by walking single file along logs laid end to end, all of which was excellent training. Near midday the column entered Mobile at the end of St. Joseph Street. They marched through Mobile until they reached Frascati Park three miles south of town on Mobile Bay. They were joined along the way by wagons and others walking and watching. The Apache soldiers put on quite a show, wheeling and pivoting with sergeants barking commands, as they went through the manual of arms. It was as entertaining as a circus parade. When the supply wagon reached the park, the command to pitch tents was given. Sixteen minutes later, the tents were up and the soldiers were waiting to draw rations. It was the only military encampment ever held by the Apaches in the eastern United States.

Lieutenant Wotherspoon had a large command tent set up and held a luncheon party for guests of the officers and other town dignitaries. In an interview, Wotherspoon explained that the march was to test the marching power of the men, and because Apaches were used to walking and not riding, it had been an easy task. (Note: Old-time Apache warriors, while excellent horsemen, were not cavalry fighters but mounted infantry—they usually dismounted to fight.) He said that they would have liberty to visit downtown Mobile, and he "earnestly requested" that no one give them intoxicating liquors, since it was a violation of federal law to sell any Indian liquor of any kind.

With liberty passes until 11:00 p.m. and money in their pockets, the soldiers went to downtown Mobile. All but two, whom the police found drunk and put in jail, returned on time. Three returned drunk but managed to do so still standing and on time. The next day, all except those drawing guard duty were given liberty until 9:00 p.m. that evening. All returned to camp on time and sober. They had bought gifts for loved ones, seen the sights, and attended plays. They said they'd had a fine time. Wotherspoon set aside the next day, Monday, March 14, for the Apaches to show off their drill training. The main event at 5:00 p.m. drew such a large crowd that it spilled over into the drill field and hampered some of the planned maneuvers. Nevertheless, the *Mobile Register* reported, "The drilling of the men was very good and they seemed to take a great deal of pride in their individual work in line."[1]

The command struck camp and was ready to depart on Tuesday morning at 7:30 a.m. but had to wait for a baker to deliver bread and other food. The men again marched through Mobile before taking the St. Stephens Road to Three Mile Creek. After a wrong turn or two, they marched to Oak Grove, a distance of twenty-one miles, by 3:00 p.m. and made camp. They were on the march again the next day at 6:30 a.m. and, despite again getting lost, had covered twenty-three miles by 2:15 p.m. and reached their camping spot at Citronelle. On Thursday, March 17, heavy rains forced them to remain in their tents. On March 18, they marched six miles before reaching the north branch of Cedar Creek. They made camp on a ridge and then spent the day building a corduroy road bridge over Cedar Creek, about five feet deep at that point. The bridge with corduroy approaches was sixty-six feet long and was completed in a little over three hours. They tested it by marching over it and driving the supply wagon over it. The following morning, the hundred-mile march was completed, and a proud commander dismissed his men at 10:30 a.m.

Lieutenant Wotherspoon provided a detailed report to his superiors at Fort Leavenworth and in Washington. He concluded with pleasure, "I report all this instruction was given with most satisfactory results. The Indians learned rapidly and readily what was taught them, conducted themselves with greater propriety than any white troops I have ever marched with, and I would not hesitate to march them anyplace after my experience. The test of camping these Indians in vicinity of a large city was certainly a thorough one and most satisfactory."[2]

The army command staff acknowledged that the march had been a big success.

George Wratten,
Friend of the Chiricahuas

GEORGE WRATTEN IS A NAME TIGHTLY WOVEN INTO THE HISTORY OF the Geronimo War and subsequent Chiricahua Apache captivity. Wratten was probably one of the best Anglo friends the Chiricahuas had, especially during their captivity; yet he is not widely known in popular histories of those times. Mickey Free and Tom Horn are probably better known as interpreters and scouts, but they were far less acceptable to Apaches than George Wratten in peace talks with the bluecoats.

Born in Sonoma, California, in 1865, George Medhurst Wratten was a son of Judge George Medhurst Wratten Sr. in San Francisco. Poor health first forced his father to move the family to Florence, Arizona, and later to establish a law practice in Albuquerque, New Mexico. When George was fourteen, he began working as a clerk in the San Carlos agency store where he had to deal with many Apache bands and their dialects and unique ways of speaking and phrasing their thoughts. Wratten apparently had a gift for understanding and speaking Apache and its dialects, getting not only the words correct but also the intent behind what was said. During his work in the agency store, he became close friends with a young warrior named Ahnandia, who stopped another Apache, angered by his treatment by the store, from slashing Wratten.[1] When Geronimo surrendered in 1886, Ahnandia and Wratten were on different sides, but they remained friends for the rest of their lives.

At fifteen, Wratten began work as a packer in General Crook's mule trains. In this job, he earned fifty dollars a month, ten dollars a month more than a second lieutenant. At sixteen, Wratten was chief of scouts

George Wratten and friend Ahnandia, 1886, Fort
Sam Houston.
COURTESY OF THE LYNDA SÁNCHEZ/EVA BALL COLLECTION

at Fort Stanton. By age twenty-one, he had served as superintendent
of General Crook's mule trains and as chief of scouts. His last service
as chief of scouts began in November 1885 when nine Apaches, under
the leadership of Ulzana, came up from Mexico to raid and provide a
bluecoat distraction while Geronimo, Naiche, and others looked for their
captive wives and ammunition for their Winchesters around San Carlos.
Over a period of five weeks, they killed thirty-eight people, rustled about

250 head of livestock—mostly mules and horses—and ranged over more than 1,200 miles. The raid led Capt. Wirt Davis to organize two additional companies of Apache scouts, A and B, each with about fifty men. Frank Bennett was chief of scouts for Company A, composed of Yuma, Tonto, and Mojave Apaches. George Wratten was chief of scouts for Company B, composed of San Carlos, White Mountain, and Coyotero Apaches. The companies served six months but were then discharged by General Miles, who had taken over from General Crook in April 1886. After leaving the army's employ in April, Wratten took a job as a part-time deputy sheriff and lived with his parents in Albuquerque. His father hoped that George would settle down and practice law with him.[1, 2]

General Nelson Miles was completely ineffective in stopping the raids of the Naiche-Geronimo band of Apaches. To save face, he took a two-pronged approach. First, he arranged to send the Chiricahuas living peaceably on the reservation to Florida. To the casual observer, this meant he was ridding Arizona of their dreaded Apaches. Second, he offered Martine and Kayihtah, two scouts who had relatives riding with the Geronimo warriors, a large monetary award if they would accompany his peace emissary to find Geronimo in Mexico and talk him into surrendering. Miles then called Lt. Charles Gatewood, who had many admirers among the Apaches for his fairness and integrity, to his headquarters in Albuquerque. At the meeting, General Miles directed Gatewood to take Martine and Kayihtah with him, find Geronimo, and offer peace terms. Gatewood, in poor health, agreed to go. Leaving the meeting, Gatewood ran into George Wratten on a street in Albuquerque and told him that he was going to look for Geronimo and offer peace terms from General Miles. Knowing Wratten's language skills, Gatewood asked him to accompany the little expedition as interpreter, and Wratten agreed. Gatewood was conversant in Apache, but he believed no mistakes would be made in interpreting what both sides said if Wratten did the interpreting. Wratten's father strongly objected to George's accepting another enlistment as chief of scouts, but the young man left with Gatewood.[2]

After five or six weeks in some of Mexico's roughest country, Gatewood and Wratten, guided by Martine and Kayihtah, found Geronimo's warriors. Martine and Kayihtah first, and Gatewood the next day, made the case for surrender. With Wratten serving as interpreter, they convinced the Apaches.

When Geronimo surrendered his rifle to Miles and made a peace agreement, he requested that Wratten be allowed to accompany them to Florida, to which Wratten and Miles agreed. As a result, Wratten's parents disowned him. His father died a few weeks later, but George was not informed of his death.

The train carrying the Geronimo band to Florida unexpectedly stopped at Fort Sam Houston in San Antonio, Texas, and the Apaches spent the next six weeks living in tents set up in the fort's quadrangle while President Grover Cleveland decided what to do with them. Wratten had his own tent among the Apaches and for some unknown reason had several rifles and ammunition with him. As the Apaches had not been told why they were stopped, rumors began circulating among them that the army planned to execute them all. Even Wratten thought this might be the case and, believing it uncalled for and unjust, told Geronimo that if shooting started, there were a few rifles and ammunition in his tent. He said Apaches should take them and defend themselves, and he would help them.

The army finally had to interview Geronimo and Naiche separately to get the straight story of Geronimo's surrender terms. George Wratten served as the interpreter at these interviews and also testified as a witness because he was there as the interpreter when Gatewood and Miles talked to the band about surrender.[3] Soon after the interviews, President Cleveland decided the Apaches were prisoners of war and sent them on to Florida. At Pensacola, the train stopped again. The warriors were taken off the train, separated from their families, and sent with George Wratten to Fort Pickens on Santa Rosa Island in Pensacola Bay. Their families were sent on to Fort Marion at Saint Augustine about 360 miles away.

At this point, Wratten's service requested by Geronimo and General Miles was complete, and he was free to return to New Mexico. However, he stayed with the Apaches. Probably because he was the only one who could easily speak their language, he was placed in immediate supervisory charge of them and reported to Lt. Charles Parker and Capt. J. E. Wilson.

Captain Wilson reported Wratten's support was necessary and valuable, saying that Wratten explained everything to the Apaches, took charge of and issued rations and clothing, and supervised their work details. According to Wilson, "He is a most excellent and reliable man in every way." At Fort Pickens, Wratten also spent much time teaching English to the Apaches. He taught Geronimo and Naiche how to write their autographs for sale. He showed Mangas how to make his mark and others how to draw Indian scenes on pieces of paper, which could be sold to the tourists allowed on the island. All this, and George Wratten was not yet twenty-two years old.

The warriors at Fort Pickens were reunited with their families about seven months after they arrived, and a year later, they all joined the rest of the Chiricahuas at Mount Vernon Barracks. Their move and reunification were no doubt helped by George Wratten, who translated their words into English and wrote the War Department and others constantly to remind them that General Miles had made promises that were not being kept. Wratten went with the band to Mount Vernon and again played a supervisory role for their work details. With help from professional carpenters, he taught them how to build houses that were much more comfortable than the log cabins they had built when they first arrived.

While at Mount Vernon Barracks, Wratten married Nah-goy-yah-kizn (kids romping and kicking), a young Apache woman who was an orphan and the niece of Lot Eyelash and Binday. She was later known as Annie White. Annie and George had two daughters, Amy, born in 1890, and Blossom, born in 1893, but Annie and George were divorced by late 1893. Annie eventually married Talbot Gooday, and they had seven children.

With his interpretive skills and knowledge of their ways and lives, George Wratten was instrumental in helping with the smooth transition of the Apaches from Mount Vernon Barracks to Fort Sill, Oklahoma, in 1894. In addition to providing interpreting services for the Chiricahua military supervisors, he provided the Chiricahuas with help in repairing machinery needed to make their farming and cattle operations functional. He also operated a store from which the Apaches could buy supplies, and he hired teenager Eugene Chihuahua, son of Chief Chihuahua and one of a few children not forced to go to the Carlisle school, and taught him to read and write by reading the labels on cans and to do arithmetic to add up store orders.[4]

George Wratten married again in 1899. His bride was Julie Cannon, whom he had met when the Apaches were at Mount Vernon. They had three sons and two daughters. They left Fort Sill to try to farm at Mount Vernon, but floods and other natural disasters made him leave that endeavor and return to Fort Sill, where he continued as an interpreter for the army until he died from a fatal back ailment on June 23, 1912, at age forty-seven. He was buried in the Fort Sill Cemetery with a brick red stone to mark his grave. Many Apaches considered him the best white friend they ever had and mourned him deeply when he passed away.

Geronimo Tries to
Fire George Wratten

GEORGE WRATTEN BECAME AN ARMY EMPLOYEE TO SUPPORT THE CARE
and management of the Apache prisoners of war and was a major stabi-
lizing influence for them. However, his work with the Apaches came at
great personal cost. When he traveled east with the Apaches, his parents,
who wanted him to become an attorney and work with his father, disowned him. He stayed with the Chiricahuas for nearly the rest of his life.
He served as the interpreter in important meetings the government had

Geronimo and George Wratten ca. 1895.
PHOTO OF GERONIMO COURTESY OF NATIONAL ARCHIVES; PHOTO OF GEORGE WRATTEN COUR-
TESY OF ARIZONA HISTORICAL SOCIETY

with the Chiricahuas and as a reliable advisor to the various commanders who were responsible for them.

By June 1888, the captive Chiricahuas were finally grouped all together at Mount Vernon Barracks, Alabama, but they continued to suffer deteriorating health from the high humidity, tuberculosis, and mosquito-borne diseases. In June 1890, Lt. William Wallace Wotherspoon was directed to take special charge of them. He first created a makeshift hospital, later a full-time facility, for the Apaches and then put the men to work clearing land, planting gardens, and building much higher-quality houses on top of a nearby ridge to replace the log-cabin hovels built in a low place near the barracks gate. Although the Mount Vernon soil was poor, the Apaches were able to grow enough vegetables for their own use and even some to sell.

In May 1891, the army created an all-Indian company, Company I, 12th Infantry, at Mount Vernon in which forty-six Chiricahuas enlisted. George Wratten continued as superintendent of the twenty-eight men who remained in camp, including Geronimo, but late in the summer of that year, Lieutenant Wotherspoon made Geronimo a judge or justice of the peace to oversee Chiricahua misdemeanor cases.

Three years later, Geronimo had gained insight into White Eye methods for dealing with legal problems, and he began to try to reassert his influence among his people. George Wratten stood in his way. The issue came to a head when Lieutenant Wotherspoon had Wratten arrest Geronimo for drunkenness and made him serve five days at hard labor. Geronimo decided to remove Wratten by replacing him with a malleable young student from Carlisle as his interpreter, and he took a legalistic approach to the removal. He was, no doubt, encouraged in this effort when Wotherspoon was transferred to New York and a new, young lieutenant, Charles Ballou, replaced him.

Geronimo asked Maj. G. B. Russell, commandant of Mount Vernon Barracks, for a hearing. Russell told him to secure witnesses, prepare his case, and bring the young Apache from Carlisle with whom he wanted to replace Wratten. Geronimo wanted the hearing to be a council meeting. Russell said no, that a general talk among Indians would be intended to show off his brilliance and receive the applause of his followers. Instead,

Russell had Geronimo call in his witnesses one at a time and have his interpreter candidate do the interpreting. All the statements were recorded.[1]

Geronimo began his case by claiming that Wratten had been his choice for interpreter and General Miles had followed his recommendation. Therefore, Wratten was serving at his discretion and being paid because of him. Wratten denied that he was paid because of Geronimo, saying he was paid by the government and took his orders from army officers. Geronimo said General Miles had told him to dismiss the interpreter when he no longer wanted him to serve. Now, Geronimo claimed, when an Indian spoke three words to Wratten, he was told to shut his mouth and go away. Geronimo said his most recent problem with Wratten occurred when he and his wife went to Wratten's house to tell him a number of Apaches were drinking and misbehaving. He wanted Wratten to tell Captain Wotherspoon to put a stop to it. He claimed that Wratten told him he couldn't tell Wotherspoon to do anything, that he, Geronimo, couldn't talk to him, and to shut up. Geronimo told Russell that he personally complained to Wotherspoon the next day about Wratten's refusal to listen to him. After Geronimo made his talk, he brought in his witnesses. Major Russell wrote that none of them said anything that had a bearing on Geronimo's charge. One had said he saw Wratten kick a drunken Indian woman.[2]

After the hearing, the allegations were submitted to Wratten in writing. He replied that he had received the statements and believed he could leave the matter in the hands of the officers who knew how he performed the work. He said it was true that many times he was compelled to tell the Indians to stop talking because it was almost impossible for most of them to confine themselves to the issue under discussion. He said if he didn't cut them off, he would be in constant council. But he pointed out that no one could say he ever refused to hear anything in reason and that the charge that he had kicked an Indian woman was false and could not be sustained by evidence.

Wratten submitted his reply to Lieutenant Ballou, who endorsed and forwarded it to Major Russell, noting, "Mr. Wratten's honesty, patience, fidelity and capability are too well known to you to require any comment from me."[2]

Major Russell made his report to Secretary of War Daniel Scott Lamont, who had recently visited the Apaches and knew the situation. The report began,

The complaint made by Geronimo was probably made in the hope of having Mr. Wratten succeeded as interpreter by one of the Apaches recently dismissed from Carlisle, Pennsylvania. . . . In my opinion, the request is not worthy of serious consideration. It seems to me that, from old age and a misapprehension of the state of affairs, Geronimo has mistakenly and falsely considered that the position of Government Interpreter was [created] *by himself and that he* [Wratten] *is there as* [his] *appointee. . . . The overseer of such an assembly of savages can hardly remain popular throughout, but I believe Mr. Wratten's truthfulness, faithfulness and care in controlling these people have been appreciated by them. I think that Geronimo feels his own authority would be increased by Wratten's removal and that this is the cause of his request.*[2]

Wotherspoon received a copy of the allegations on May 8. Three days later, he forwarded the report with his opinion strongly supporting Major Russell's conclusions to Capt. George W. Davis in Secretary Lamont's office. Wotherspoon, who would one day be general of the army, said that during his long army career he had never known a more honest or fearless man than Wratten; nor had he seen anyone whose judgment in dealing with Indians was sounder. He functioned as more than a mere interpreter; he was a skilled farmer and an excellent mechanic, carpenter, and smith. His knowledge of Apache character had been of the greatest value in training them in captivity.

On May 14, Adjutant General Robert P. Hughes answered Major Russell's report. Part of the letter was directed to Geronimo. He was told that Secretary Lamont had read the charges and considered them frivolous; Wratten was to be retained in his present position as long as he performed satisfactorily, and he was in no sense an appointee of the Apaches or subject to their will or control. The Apaches would be treated with justice, and every reasonable request would be granted if possible. Furthermore, Geronimo was not recognized by the government as a chief or entitled to any more consideration than any other Indian of his tribe.[3]

Hughes's message was a hard blow to Geronimo's ego. He continued to make unfair comments about Wratten. However, to their credit, when they traveled to big events in cities and expositions in the future and Wratten was Geronimo's interpreter on those trips, they put aside their animosity. When they fought, it was with little more than "loaded epithets."

Chiricahua Prisoners Make Their
Case for a Move, August 29, 1894

By late 1893, the Saint Augustine Fort Marion Chiricahua Apaches had been at Mount Vernon Barracks, Alabama, over six years, and those from Pensacola, Fort Pickens, over five years. The army had moved them there to give them more space, to reunite the Fort Pickens Apaches with the rest of the tribe, and to provide a more healthful climate. But Mount Vernon was surrounded by dense forests and swamps that allowed little air movement, making the heat and humidity insufferable. Torrential rains came often, and clouds of mosquitos spread malaria and yellow fever. The Apaches were at Mount Vernon less than a year before army leadership began to realize they needed to be moved. Their death rate was still three times the national average, and the land was too poor for them to farm.

Congress and the bureaucrats in Washington tried to destroy tribal culture through the Dawes Act (among other things, assigning a fixed acreage to each Indian and taking back the rest of the reservation), education of young children far from their parents, and making the adults disappear into "clearly superior" white society through farming and manual trades. At Mount Vernon, the Chiricahuas made the best of a bad situation by learning carpentry, becoming soldiers, and letting their children be locally taught White Eye knowledge, while the Chiricahuas continued to tell their children tribal history and stories and conducted important tribal ceremonies such as the puberty ceremony for girls to become young women. The Chiricahuas had learned enough about

Participants in the August 1894 meeting between army representatives and Chiricahua leaders. Around the circle beginning at 10:00 and moving clockwise: Geronimo, Naiche, Chihuahua, Nana, Chatto, Kaytennae, Loco, Mangas; in the center, L–R: Lt. Hugh L. Scott, Capt. Marion P. Maus.
BACKGROUND PHOTO BY JOHN FOWLER, COURTESY OF NATIONAL ARCHIVES; INDIVIDUAL PHOTOS COURTESY OF NATIONAL ARCHIVES AND LIBRARY OF CONGRESS

White Eye culture to survive as a tribe, and they badly wanted to get away from Mount Vernon.

After over four years of political wrangling in Congress and between Congress and War Department bureaucrats, the War Department decided in late 1893 to try a second time to relocate the prisoners. It had tried after Crook's 1890 report but was stopped by congressional politics. The North Carolina mountains on and near the Cherokee reservation suggested by Crook didn't have enough arable land to make Chiricahua farms self-sufficient. By August 6, 1894, the War Department had managed to get an amendment to the Army Appropriations Act, authorizing the transfer of the Chiricahuas to any military reservation under its control. The War Department then considered a plan to distribute them to various locations around the country with the restriction that they could not be sent to Texas, Arizona, or New Mexico. The plan was sent to General Miles, who was in charge of the Department of Missouri, providing oversight to the eastern half of the western military posts. Miles opposed the policy saying that it would be a "gross injustice and refined cruelty to separate family and friends." He suggested all the Chiricahuas be moved to Fort Sill and sent Lt. Hugh Lenox Scott (stationed at Fort Sill) and Capt. Marion P. Maus (on his staff) to confer with the Apaches at Mount Vernon on their preferences.[1]

The Comanches and Kiowas living around Fort Sill, and to whom the land would revert when the army left, learned of the proposed move and held a council with Scott, whom they knew and trusted and had named Sign Talker because he understood and could speak the universal sign language of the Plains Indians. They told Scott that, although they had never liked the Apaches, they would accept them there as long as they stayed on Fort Sill land, which was a typical display of Indian sympathy for homeless people.

Maus and Scott arrived at Mount Vernon Barracks and held their conference on August 29, 1894. Second Lieutenant Allyn Capron, who was then in charge of the Chiricahuas at Mount Vernon, and George Wratten, serving as interpreter, attended. Lieutenant Scott recorded the proceedings. The Apaches were asked their wishes about being moved to some other locality. They had already met together earlier to form their answer and selected Geronimo as their speaker, who, in straightforward language, summarized how they felt. Geronimo said,

I'm very glad to hear you talk. I've been wanting for a long time to hear somebody talk that way. I want to go away somewhere where we can get a farm, cattle, and cool water.

I've done my best to help the authorities—to keep peace and good order to keep my house clean. God hears both of us, and what he hears must be the truth. We're very thankful to you—these poor people who have nothing and nothing to look forward to—what you say makes my head and whole body feel cool. We're all that way. We want to see things growing around our houses, corn, and flowers. We all want it. We want you to talk for us to General Miles in the same way you have talked to us.

Young men, old men, women, and children all want to get away from here. It's too hot and wet. Too many of us die here. I remember what I told General Miles—I told him that I wanted to be a good man as long as I live, and I've done it so far. I stood up on my feet and held my hands up to God to witness what I said was true. I feel good about what you say, and it will make all the other Indians feel good. Every one of us have got children at school, and we'll behave ourselves on account of these children; we want them to learn. I don't consider that I'm an Indian any more. I'm a white man, and we'd like to go around and see different places. I consider all white men are my brothers and all white women are now my sisters. That is all I want to say. [Crook, in his day, would have called his last assertion of whiteness another Geronimo lie, but the next fifteen years would prove Geronimo's sincerity.]¹

Maus said, "I understand it to be your opinion that all of you want to go somewhere."

Geronimo answered, "We all want to go, everybody."

Naiche said, "We live just like white people, have houses and stoves just like them, and we want to have farms just like other white people. We've been here a long time and haven't seen any of us have a farm yet."

Chihuahua said, "God made the earth for everybody, and I want a piece of it. I want to have things growing. I want the wind to blow on me just as it blows on everybody else. I want the sun to shine on me and the moon, just as everybody else." Remembering his children, he said, "I went to Carlisle to see them, and it made my heart feel good to see them in the white man's road. . . . I want to have all our children together where I can see them. I want my children wherever I go." Remembering when Maus brought him back to Fort Bowie from his March 1886 meeting with General Crook as a hostile, he said, "I want you to look at me and see that I'm not like I was when you saw me before."

Nana said that, although he was too old to work, he wanted "to see young men have a farm, and I could go around and talk to them and get something to eat."

Chatto said, "If anything I could say would hurry up the farms, I wish it would. You can find some of the old people yet, the grandmothers and grandfathers, but most of them are dead. That's why I don't like it here. I want to hurry. I want you to tell General Miles to get them away from here in a hurry."

Kaytennae said, "I had lots of friends, cousins, brothers, and relatives when you saw me, but since coming to this country, they have all died— have children here and all the time afraid that they will get sick and die."

Loco said, "It's just like a road with a precipice on both sides—they fall off on both sides—nobody killed them. Sickness did it."

Mangas said, "When I got there [Fort Pickens], I have been a good man and have never stepped off the good path. While walking around I always want to look pleasant at everybody. . . . Here we are in this little bit of reservation—there are lots of trees here, yes—they shade but when you put your foot on the ground it burns you."

As Scott remembered it later, some of the prisoners told him Mount Vernon was no larger than a thumbnail and the trees were so thick one had to climb to the top of a tall pine to see the sun. He told them that they would be sent to a place where they could not only look up at the sun but also see mountains.

General Miles sent their statements along with his recommendations to the War Department, and it was officially decided the Chiricahuas would be sent to Fort Sill. There, they would still be prisoners of war.

A month before the move to Fort Sill, tragedy struck Geronimo's life once more. On September 9, 1894, his grown son Chappo died. Geronimo had tried to save Chappo from army execution, which he was certain might happen at any time, and from disease (malaria, yellow fever, and tuberculosis) sweeping through Fort Marion that could infect anyone at any time. Geronimo thought the safest way to save Chappo was by sending the young man, eager for White Eye knowledge, away to school at Carlisle. Chappo was sent to Carlisle after the move to Mount Vernon, but before he could finish his studies, he was sent back home a few months before he died of tuberculosis that had infected him at Carlisle. Chappo's body was sent via train to the national cemetery at Mobile, and Geronimo, his wife Zi-yeh, and a second woman, probably Geronimo's grown daughter, Chappo's sister, Dohn-say, accompanied it. Chappo's mother, Chee-hash-kish, if she still lived, was a slave somewhere in Mexico.

PART IV

PRISONERS OF WAR AT FORT SILL, OKLAHOMA

The Chiricahuas were shipped to Fort Sill, Oklahoma, on October 4, 1894. They arrived too late in the season to build houses and with little more than the clothes on their backs. That first winter they lived in canvas-covered wickiups and worked cutting wood for fence posts and housing lumber. They resided and prospered on the military reservation for eighteen years before they were released as prisoners of war, and the majority moved west to settle on the Mescalero reservation in the Sacramento Mountains of central New Mexico. Those who didn't want to leave their eighteen-year investment of life in Oklahoma stayed and were given farms around the town of Apache, about twenty miles northwest of Fort Sill. Both groups continued to consider themselves Chiricahua Apaches despite government attempts to destroy tribal culture through the Dawes Act of 1887 and the Indian Reorganization Act of 1934.

The Chiricahua Prisoners of War Go to Fort Sill, Oklahoma

Lieutenant Hugh L. Scott, stationed at Fort Sill, learned that the post commander was angry at the prospect of having to deal with Apache prisoners of war and planned to build a palisaded pen and corral in which to keep them under guard. Scott knew this approach had the makings of a major disaster and would drive the prisoners to run away. The war that would follow hunting them out of their native mountains

Chiricahua lodges at Fort Sill, winter of 1894–1895.
COURTESY OF NATIONAL ARCHIVES

would be worse than anything seen before as the Apaches, having lived as prisoners for eight years, would never again surrender. They would fight to the last man. Scott managed to get word to Gen. Nelson Miles of what the commander planned. Miles went over the commander's head, putting Scott in charge of the Apaches and transferring the commander.

The Apaches were moved to Fort Sill on October 4, 1894. A special train carried the Chiricahua prisoners by way of New Orleans and Fort Worth to Rush Springs, Oklahoma, about thirty miles east of Fort Sill. The capable and humane Lt. Allyn Capron, their commander at Mount Vernon Barracks, accompanied them and stayed at Fort Sill to help Lieutenant Scott with their supervision. George Wratten continued as their interpreter and operated their post supply store once things were settled.[1]

At stops along the way to Rush Springs, Geronimo, the subject of numerous newspaper articles, received cheers and ovations much to the disgust of Oklahomans, many of whom called him a murderer and said, "The old devil should have been hanged fifteen years ago." A separate train freight car carried most of the Chiricahuas' few belongings, including windows and doors and some lumber from their houses in Mount Vernon, but these were destroyed by fire in a train shed in New Orleans.

At Rush Springs, 296 wearied and bedraggled Apaches stepped from the train to climb onto wagons waiting to carry them west to Fort Sill. These didn't include the forty-five students still at Carlisle. The travelers had a few trunks and boxes but no livestock or even dogs or cats. Hundreds of Comanches and Kiowas came to meet them and tried to talk to them in the universal sign language used on the plains. But the Apaches, rarely having been on the plains, didn't understand it. Scott took some Kiowa Apaches to try to communicate with them, but their dialect was too far removed from that of the Chiricahuas to be understood. Finally, both sides produced boys from each tribe who spoke their parents' language and had learned to speak English at Carlisle. Thus, communications were established between the tribes with English as the mediating language.

As had been the case at Fort Pickens and Mount Vernon Barracks, the men worked under army command. By the time Chiricahuas arrived at Fort Sill, it was too late in the year to build houses. As a result, they built wickiups in the brush along Medicine Bluff Creek and Cache Creek and used army canvas supplied by Scott to cover their shelters.[2]

The Shepard sisters who had taught the Chiricahua children at Mount Vernon were willing to go to Fort Sill, but the War Department wouldn't pay their salaries, and their sponsors decided against sending them. As a result, arrangements were made with the Indian Office to send the children to the Plains tribes' boarding school at Anadarko, Oklahoma, thirty-three miles to the northeast. Scott gathered the parents one evening around a big fire and told them wagons would be ready in four days to carry their children to the boarding school at Anadarko and that he wanted the children to be clean, neat, and ready to start. He looked around the assembled parents, but not a word was said. He asked Chihuahua if he had anything to say. Chihuahua answered that of course they didn't want to see their children taken to a boarding school far from them, but they had been there long enough to know that the officer's orders were carried out. The children would be ready. During the school term, the children's mothers would take them candy or other treats and trot the sixty-six-mile round-trip to see their children.

Soon after the Chiricahuas arrived at Fort Sill, they learned that a grove of mesquite trees grew to the southwest about forty-five miles away. Mesquite beans and pods were among their favorite foods, and they had not had any since their imprisonment nearly eight years earlier. They asked Scott for permission to go gather the mesquite beans. He let them go, provided they left after noon on Saturday and were back ready to work by 7:00 a.m. on the following Monday. They took a few horses to carry tents, supplies, and beans on their return and trotted the distance to the mesquite grove. After gathering about three hundred bushels of beans, they trotted the forty-five miles back and were ready for work on time on Monday morning.

For the Chiricahua move to Fort Sill, Congress had appropriated money to buy a herd of cattle, but the money had to be used quickly, or it would revert to the treasury. The Fort Sill land was unfenced. There was no time to fence it or to raise winter feed, and if the cattle drifted on to Comanche-Kiowa land, bad feelings could be expected from the Comanche-Kiowas when the Chiricahua cattle ate their grass and from the Chiricahua when the Comanche-Kiowas made steak suppers from their cattle. This meant the cattle had to be herded to stay on Fort Sill land and that the Apaches had to learn cowboy skills. Scott and Capron, learning from soldiers who had been cowboys, were on constant duty teaching the Apaches how to cowboy and supervise the herd. They found it necessary to stay close to the herd, and that meant sleeping in Apache camps. Other officers advised them not to do that, saying the Apaches would cut their throats while they slept and escape, but they stayed with the Apaches and slept as safely as if they were in their own beds.

Of much public concern was the fear that the Apaches would leave Fort Sill and break away for their mountain homeland in eastern Arizona and Mexico. Scott talked with a Mescalero who was living with the Comanches and knew all the trails and waterholes along the seven hundred miles to the Mescalero agency. He had a good map drawn up with the Mescalero's information and sent a copy to General Miles to prepare him for instant action. Additionally, he kept a twenty-day supply of rations and a pack outfit ready to use. He gathered his prisoners, told them of his preparations, and warned them that the Comanches, who knew the plains, were his friends, not theirs, and would join him in pursuing the Chiricahuas if they left. The Apaches never considered breaking away from Fort Sill.

Apache Prisoner of War
Life at Fort Sill

WITH THE COMING OF SPRING IN 1895, THE MILITARY COMMANDER FOR the Chiricahuas at Fort Sill, Capt. Hugh Lenox Scott, who was promoted from lieutenant in January 1895, let the Chiricahuas organize into small villages of related groups, as was the old Apache custom, along Cache Creek and Medicine Bluff Creek. Headmen, who held the position through recognized natural leadership and not through some arbitrary bureaucratic appointment, supervised the villages. The list of

Geronimo's wife, Zi-yeh; his grandchildren Nina and Thomas Dahkeya; Eva, his daughter with Zi-yeh; and Geronimo in their pumpkin-and-melon patch at Fort Sill, ca. 1895.
COURTESY OF LIBRARY OF CONGRESS

headmen reads like a Chiricahua *Who's Who*: Geronimo, Kayihtah, Perico, Chihuahua, Noche, Kaytennae, Mangas, Toclanny, Loco, Naiche, Chatto, and an unknown in prominent names, Tom Chiricahua.[1, 2]

The villages were far enough apart for privacy but within easy walking distance of each other. The men, who had learned carpentry and how to build good, snug houses at Mount Vernon, began to build "picket" houses (upright posts set in a frame) for the villages. The house design included a covered breezeway, large enough to drive a wagon through, between two enclosed sections. All three components were covered with a single roof, which was a common design for houses on the prairie.

Captain Scott and Lt. Allyn Capron were active in helping the Apaches reestablish their lives. Scott was able to find mules as army surplus when Fort Supply in Oklahoma was closed. He gave them to the Apaches and directed them in breaking out land and cultivating it. Each man had a plot of his own for gardens and crops. That first year they raised more than 250,000 melons and cantaloupes. They ate what they could and sold the rest at the post. Scott's nine-year-old daughter is said to have worked at their wagons, bargaining prices and making change. Scott, having seen normally used varieties of corn crops destroyed by scorching southwestern winds, had the Apaches plant a new grain sorghum, Kaffir corn, from the dry plains of Africa, which was in enthusiastic use by Kansas farmers. The Kaffir corn grown by the Chiricahuas was the first in Oklahoma. Its fodder furnished feed for the Apache livestock, and the excess was sold to the post. They also cut and baled hay from the thin prairie grass and sold what they didn't use to the government. And they cut posts and purchased wire to build a cattle fence around the post and the villages, eliminating the need to keep continuous watch on the cattle herd.[3]

Asa Daklugie, Geronimo's nephew, returned to his people at Fort Sill in 1895 after spending over eight years as a student at Carlisle. At Carlisle, he had learned cattle husbandry after deciding that raising cattle was the best and only work for men who could no longer support themselves through raiding and hunting. Upon his arrival, he looked over the Apache cattle still being herded to keep them within the Fort Sill boundary and saw their poor quality and apparent problems. He went to George Wratten, manager of their trading post, who did some of the hiring. He told Wratten of his years of cattle study and how the herd should be improved. Wratten sent him to Captain Scott. Daklugie let Scott know in no uncertain terms his dissatisfaction with conditions for the Apaches at Fort Sill and got into a scuffle with Scott, who was a small man and no match for the much larger Daklugie. Scott dashed from his office, mounted his horse, and rode away.

Daklugie sat down to wait for the military police. He waited for over an hour, and when no police arrived, he mounted his pony and rode to the trading post, where Wratten told him that Scott had stopped there and wanted to know who the ruffian was who wanted to run the reservation. Wratten said Scott had listened as he told him about who Daklugie was, his background, his intention to marry Ramona Chihuahua, and his desire for a job. Wratten went on to tell Scott, "He may dislike you, and you, him. But to an Apache, respect is more important than liking. There is no real friendship without it." After hearing Wratten out, the captain put Daklugie in charge of the cattle. Scott admitted that although there were some good cowboys among the Apaches, their overall management had been inefficient. When Daklugie saw Captain Scott again, it was in his office. Scott stood, and they shook hands. Daklugie had come to ask for some good bulls, and Scott approved the purchase. By the time the Apaches sold the herd in 1913 before leaving for Mescalero, it was considered one of the best in Oklahoma.

Apaches still serving in the army when the prisoners of war were sent to Fort Sill went with them and continued to serve out their enlistment terms. By the summer of 1895, sixty-seven Apaches were still enlisted at Fort Sill. They had been merged with twenty-three Comanches in Troop L of the Seventh Cavalry to serve until their enlistments were up. Captain Scott said they were excellent in drill, reliable on guard details, and able to maintain order in the Apache camps and keep illegal Anglo cattlemen and traders off the reservation. However, much of their time was spent learning various tradecrafts. In May 1897, the Indian company at Fort Sill held its last drill. Twelve of the Apaches were able to reenlist as scouts. Few of the others were able to find work near the post and were soon starving. The army neither helped them find work nor allowed them to leave Fort Sill as free men. There were still army officers who were strongly biased against them, and their six years of excellent service had not changed their attitudes. General Otis Howard observed that some men resisted the idea that in the future they might be taking orders from an Apache sergeant.

The old, great Apache leaders passed away at Fort Sill. Nana died in 1896, Chihuahua and Mangas in 1901, Loco in 1905, and Geronimo in 1909. Many credit the passing of Geronimo as the tipping point in the government's decision to free the prisoners of war. During his years of breaking out of the San Carlos and Fort Apache reservations, the frontier press had blamed Geronimo for every attack on Anglos by the Apaches regardless of the possibility that he had not been within five hundred miles.

At Fort Sill, Geronimo became the most famous of the Apache prisoners. His signed souvenirs were sought after and sold in nearby Lawton and at the post. He was much in demand for newspaper interviews. In 1898, he went to his first big commercial attraction, the Trans-Mississippi and International Exposition in Omaha. Soon he was in demand for other fairs and exhibitions, such as the 1904 Louisiana Purchase Exposition in Saint Louis. In 1905, Geronimo, Quanah Parker, and four other great warrior chiefs from the Plains tribes were invited to ride in Theodore Roosevelt's inaugural parade. Lieutenant George Purington, military commander of the Apaches at Fort Sill, gave Geronimo a check for $171 to cover expenses for the trip, including shipment of his best horse. Geronimo cashed the check at the local bank, kept one dollar, and deposited the rest before leaving on his trip to Washington. When he returned, his pockets were stuffed with cash, and he had a trunk filled with new clothes. When he passed away in 1909, it's said that he had over $10,000 (about $276,000 in today's coin) in a bank account.

Geronimo on the Army Payroll

FOR NEARLY THIRTY-FIVE YEARS, GERONIMO FOUGHT AND KILLED Mexicans without mercy. He was actually captured once (by John Clum and his scouts), broke out of the Chokonen, San Carlos, and Fort Apache reservations a total of four times, and left long trails of death, fire, and destruction wherever he went before he surrendered to an army commander, who then returned him to a reservation. Geronimo was probably the most feared Indian war leader in the United States.

By the time Geronimo surrendered to General Miles in 1886, 25 percent of the entire army was chasing him and spending hundreds of thousands of dollars a year in its efforts. Upon surrender, the band of warriors Geronimo had led in war was sent to prisoner of war camps first in Florida, then Alabama, and finally Oklahoma. Given the blood and treasure the army had spent to ultimately bring Geronimo and his Chiricahuas under control, it was extraordinary that, less than five years after surrendering, Geronimo, a prisoner of war, was on the army's payroll.

In early May 1891, Lt. William W. Wotherspoon, army commander of the Chiricahua prisoners of war at Mount Vernon Barracks (and future chief of staff of the army), had enlisted forty-six Chiricahua men (including five or six from the Carlisle Indian school) to be part of Company I of the 12th Infantry along with thirty-one Apaches who had enlisted and were brought from San Carlos. Wotherspoon reported that Geronimo, who was too old to enlist, felt badly slighted, "so he will be given special work to pacify him."

By September 1891, Wotherspoon had appointed Geronimo as justice of the peace, or judge, for the Apache village. Geronimo wore a uniform as a symbol of his leading importance, and Lieutenant Wotherspoon paid him out of a special fund a monthly salary of $10.50. Geronimo's pay

Geronimo in uniform as an army scout, head of his village, Fort Sill, Oklahoma, ca. 1898. *Chief Geronimo Apache* painting by Elbridge Ayer Burbank, part of the Chiricahua–Fort Sill, Oklahoma, Oil on Canvas Collection.

as a judge continued until the Chiricahuas were transferred to Fort Sill in early October 1894. Since Geronimo was not in the army but was more like a modern civil servant, his supervisor was George Wratten, who had been given responsibility for the Chiricahua men who had not enlisted.[1]

As soon as the first winter passed at Fort Sill, Capt. Hugh Scott, commander of the Chiricahuas at Fort Sill, set the men to building houses. The men built seventy-one houses distributed over the reservation in twelve small villages of four to eight houses for family groupings; a headman for each was suggested by the interpreter George Wratten but agreed to by the village. Captain Scott followed nearly all Wratten's suggestions for village leaders, which included Geronimo. That first year in 1895, the seventy-one Chiricahua families raised over 250,000 melons and cantaloupes (about 3,500 per acre) on previously untilled soil. Geronimo was one of the best farmers.

Village headman was not a position the army had on its list of specialties. Therefore, Captain Scott had the headmen enlist for the first three-year period as soldiers, entitled to wear the army uniform and draw the pay of privates, even if many of them had passed the age of active service. As privates, the village headmen all received uniforms and had to maintain them in good repair for weekly inspections, and the villages were inspected to ensure the houses were taken care of and cleanliness maintained.[2]

As a headman drawing army pay, Geronimo saw himself as a soldier enlisted in the US Army. When nearly all the Fort Sill soldiers left in 1898 to fight in the Spanish-American War, unfounded panic over a rumor that the Apaches were holding war dances and that Geronimo was going to lead a breakout and murder everyone spread like wildfire. Fortunately, clear heads and a few soldiers sent back from boarding the train at Rush Springs, Oklahoma, to fight in the Spanish-American War calmed the situation, and normal day-to-day life quickly returned. Jason Betzinez, who as a young man rode with Geronimo and then went to the Carlisle school after the surrender, lived at Fort Sill and said that Geronimo was very disturbed by the story because he was then an American soldier and wearing the uniform. Thus, in an ironic twist of fate, Geronimo, the dreaded Apache war leader, became Geronimo, private, US Army, who had to defend his status as a soldier against rumors of his planned depredations as an Apache.

Eldridge Ayer Burbank
Paints Geronimo

By 1897, THE CHIRICAHUAS HAD SETTLED INTO LIFE AT FORT SILL. They lived in picket houses in twelve villages, each with a headman of its own choosing. Each family grew eight acres of Kaffir corn, an acre of cotton, and an acre of vegetables. They had an improving and increasing cattle herd, and they had put fences around the Fort Sill land and their villages to keep cattle on the reservation and out of their villages. They dug wells, made ponds, and celebrated tribal ceremonies. The Apaches had been brought to Fort Sill for the better climate, and they were much happier there, but diseases they brought from the swamps continued to kill them at an alarming rate, and no one understood why. So it was in 1897 that Geronimo's sixteen- or seventeen-year-old son Fenton, whose mother was Zi-yeh, died in the spring of that year.

In 1897 the White Eyes began to understand Geronimo was much more than the bloodthirsty, torture-hungry Apache described in the popular press, which claimed he had a blanket made of one hundred white scalps he had taken during his last breakout. Such claims were absurd since Apaches rarely, if ever, took scalps. Writers for major publications, who should have known better, puzzled Geronimo when they asked to see the scalp blanket. As national interest built around the fierce warrior in army captivity, Edward E. Ayer, president of the Field Museum in Chicago, sent his artist nephew, Eldridge Ayer Burbank, to Fort Sill to paint a portrait of Geronimo. Having read newspaper accounts of the "bloodthirsty savage," Burbank was glad Geronimo was in prison behind bars, where he, Burbank, could safely paint him.

Geronimo as sketched by Eldridge Ayer Burbank at Fort Sill, Oklahoma, 1897.
COURTESY OF THE NATIONAL MUSEUM OF THE AMERICAN INDIAN

Burbank arrived at Fort Sill and, upon asking to be taken to Geronimo's cell, was told the old man lived in his own house and was free to go anywhere on the reservation. A young Indian boy (probably Geronimo's grandson Thomas Dahkeya) guided Burbank to Geronimo's house, where they learned he was out hunting his horses. They waited in the breezeway until he came riding up. He first impressed Burbank as "an elderly Indian . . . short, but well-built and muscular. His keen, shrewd face was deeply furrowed with strong lines. His small black eyes were watery, but in them there burned a fierce light." The artist saw the face, "so gnarled and furrowed," as a wonderful study.[1]

Burbank greeted Geronimo with courtesy as "Chief Geronimo." Geronimo was not a chief, but he was pleased to hear it. Soldiers had nicknamed him "Gerry," which he hated. Although Geronimo then had a good understanding of English, he was slow to speak it for fear of making funny errors or causing misunderstandings and had Thomas serve as an interpreter. Geronimo asked where Burbank was from and proceeded to give him the third degree about the details of Chicago once he had an answer.

When Geronimo was satisfied that he had learned enough about Chicago, he said, "Come," and led Burbank inside the house, where he pulled a picture (probably like ones he had sold as souvenirs to passengers when trains stopped at Mount Vernon) out of an old trunk, gave it to Burbank, and said, "One dollar." Burbank grinned, paid the dollar, and then explained that he wanted to paint Geronimo's portrait and needed him to sit while he sketched and painted. Geronimo thought that was a fine idea but said Burbank had to get Captain Scott's approval first because sitting would take him away from work he was supposed to be doing.

Captain Scott approved Geronimo's sitting for the painter, and Burbank returned the next day with his art supplies to find Geronimo ready. For the first portrait, Geronimo sat on his bed, and Burbank sat on a crate Geronimo found for him. Burbank had barely started his first sketch for the painting when Geronimo signaled him to stop and called in Eva, who was playing nearby, to interpret for them.

The child said, "This man wants to know how much you're going to pay him." Burbank replied, "Ask him how much he wants."

Geronimo said through Eva, "You get much money for that picture, maybe five dollars. I want half."

Burbank said, "If you'll sit for two pictures, you can have all the five dollars." Geronimo thought it was a good bargain, and Burbank was soon back to work making sketches that would be turned into color portraits. It wasn't long before Geronimo suggested that if Burbank would buy him a chair, he, Burbank, would be a lot more comfortable in his work, and it wasn't many days before Geronimo had his chair.

Geronimo's years of being still while waiting for game or watching for raiding opportunities made him a good subject for the artist, but when Geronimo heard the least sound of man or horse approaching, he reflexively was up and at the door to see what had made the noise. Sometimes, when he had posed for a long time, Burbank let him rest on his bed, and Geronimo would sing in his deep, rich voice, according to the artist, songs "of great beauty." According to a translation Burbank had made of one such song, the words were:

> *O, ha le*
> *O, ha le*
> *Through the air*
> *I fly upon a cloud*
> *Toward the sky, far, far, far*
> *O, ha le*
> *O, ha le*
> *There to find the holy place*
> *Ah, now the change comes o'er me*
> *O, ha le*
> *O, ha le.*[2]

When Burbank worked at Geronimo's house, he brought his lunch and usually had extra to share with the old man. Once during the early sittings, Geronimo invited Burbank to eat with him, and Zi-yeh put a board between them while they sat on the floor facing each other. She served meat, bread (perhaps mesquite bread she had made from pods the Apaches had gathered from a thicket forty-five miles away to the southwest), and coffee. Burbank said the food was "clean and good" served on the board, and they ate with their fingers. Two years later, Geronimo again invited Burbank to dinner, with Zi-yeh and Eva joining them to sit at a table covered with a linen cloth for a fine meal ending with dessert. By this time, Geronimo had been to the Trans-Mississippi and International Exposition in Omaha in September and October 1898 and had made a nice profit for his labors.

Burbank, painting Geronimo in his home, saw a domestic side of the old warrior that few knew. Geronimo trained his ponies to come at his shrill note, and he never left home without putting a saucer of milk out for his cat. For some reason Burbank never understood, Geronimo kept the cat's whiskers closely clipped. Burbank also agreed to write letters for Geronimo that he dictated to friends in New Mexico or Arizona requesting "medicines" they could gather there. He always closed with, "If you're in need, let me know, and I'll send you money."

One day Burbank saw the kindly old man turn ferocious. A magazine editor offered Burbank a princely sum if he could get the story of Geronimo's life for a magazine article. Geronimo agreed to tell it for half the proceeds. Burbank prepared to write as Geronimo, lying on his bed, began, but when he got to the Mexican slaughter of his family, he arose out of his bed with such fury that he was unable to continue. The boy who was interpreting became almost as excited and said, "He's telling you the truth, for my father tells me the same story."[2] Burbank apparently never completed the article.

Burbank also saw gambling bring out Geronimo's fierceness upon accompanying him to a sports meet, probably a Fourth of July celebration at Fort Sill that included horse races and other contests with soldiers, Apaches, Comanches, and Kiowas. Geronimo wound up playing in a game of monte, dealing the cards like an expert with his small, quick hands and giving wild whoops as he raked in his winnings.

As they were leaving the celebration, a cowboy proposed they race horses for a ten-dollar bet. Geronimo liked nothing better than a good horse race, but his weight was a disadvantage if he rode, so he often won races with Zi-yeh riding for him. This day, she apparently wasn't at the festivities. Geronimo looked for an Apache boy he knew rode well and found him at bat in a baseball game. Just as Geronimo arrived, the boy hit a homer, and the old man, thinking he was trying to get away from him, chased him around the diamond and caught up with the boy at home plate. The horse race that followed was close, but Geronimo's pony won. Burbank said Geronimo was wildly exultant.

Burbank made trips to Fort Sill in 1897, 1898, and 1899. He became close friends with Geronimo and made some of the most memorable paintings and sketches of the Chiricahuas in captivity, including those of Geronimo, Eva Geronimo, and Naiche, who, a superb natural artist in his own right, watched and learned painting from Burbank.

The Chiricahua Breakout
Panic at Fort Sill

By 1898, most of the Chiricahuas had been held as prisoners of war by the army for over twelve years. The War Department could not get the Department of Interior, home of the Bureau of Indian Affairs, to take responsibility for them. All but Geronimo and Naiche's warriors, Mangas and his warrior Goso, had served more or less a year in Florida at Fort Marion and were then sent to Mount Vernon Barracks

The Apaches! painting by Fredrick Remington, ca. 1900

in Alabama. Geronimo and Naiche's band and their families served an additional year at Fort Pickens before being sent to join the others at Mount Vernon, where they lived for six years before all were transferred to Fort Sill, Oklahoma.

The Chiricahuas' move to Fort Sill was fought in Congress for four years. There was tremendous pressure to let white settlers take over Indian land in Oklahoma, and the white settlers were certain that the Apaches would again begin their deadly raids as they had in New Mexico and Arizona. Part of the congressional fight to let the Apaches settle in the Indian Nations in Oklahoma resulted from the Dawes Act passed in 1887. The Dawes Act was intended to eliminate or reduce the size of the reservations and included language that specifically said no Indians from the Southwest could have a reservation there. The War Department got around the law by sending the Apaches to Fort Sill army post lands, which covered more than 27,000 acres, and which the Comanches and Kiowas agreed to let the Apaches have after the army abandoned the post and the land reverted back to them. After arriving at Fort Sill, the Chiricahuas worked hard for the next three and a half years building houses and villages, planting ten acres of crops per family, stringing miles of fence, developing a cattle herd, learning cowboy skills to manage the cattle, digging wells, and making ponds. They were all peaceful and minded their own business.

Captain Hugh Lenox Scott, the first commander of the Fort Sill Apaches, left for a new assignment in 1897. Lieutenant Allyn K. Capron followed him as the Chiricahua prisoner commander. The Apaches respected both Scott and Capron.

In 1898, the United States became embroiled in a war with Spain. The Apaches volunteered to go fight the Spanish with Lieutenant Capron, but the army turned them down. Capron left Fort Sill early in the spring of 1898 and a few months later was the first American army officer to die in the Spanish-American War. Lieutenant Francis Beach, new to the work but anxious to treat the Apaches well, had become the commander of the Chiricahuas when Capron left. By the spring of 1898, things were so peaceful at Fort Sill that the army decided to send all but twenty soldiers stationed there to fight in Cuba. The twenty soldiers left behind were to guard supplies and perform administrative duties under Lieutenant Beach.

When the Apaches learned that Lieutenant Capron and all but twenty soldiers were leaving, their leaders held a council and discussed what they should do and expect while the soldiers were gone. They decided to hold a tribal dance that used clowns and Mountain Spirit dancers and to offer ceremonies to Ussen to protect the tribe while the soldiers were gone.

Grown Chiricahua children who had spent more than half their lives as students at Carlisle and then returned to their parents at Fort Sill watched their people with concern. They didn't understand what their elders were trying to accomplish. An "educated" Indian woman told Lieutenant Beach the Chiricahuas were "making medicine and holding war dances." Beach asked George Wratten, who as an interpreter and trading post operator had been with the Apaches since the 1886 surrender, to investigate what was going on in the Apache villages. After a quick check, Wratten reported that there was some unrest and a probability of an "attempt to escape to Arizona." He likely drew this conclusion from stories about what was said at the council when the leaders were considering their plans. Lieutenant Beach became seriously worried that there might be an attack and a breakout by the Chiricahuas.

The Fort Sill soldiers headed for Cuba on April 19, 1898. They had barely disappeared over the horizon before rumors of an impending Apache uprising to murder everyone and ride for Arizona and New Mexico started sprouting up like toadstools after a thunderstorm. There was also a story that once the troopers were gone, Comanches intended to attack the Chiricahuas in order to take back their land. Soldier families were in a near panic. A soldier's child, Mattie Morris, later reported that the families were convinced that "Geronimo and his band would harm us, as they were held prisoners on the reservation." She further said that on one occasion, "all the women and children were sent to the old guard house. My mother took us children and stayed all night." Grace Paulding, an officer's wife, wrote, "This looked to wily old Geronimo as a heaven-sent opportunity to make one last stand for freedom" and show his "defiance of his captors by massacring" what remained of the garrison.

She reported, "It was late morning when the rumor started. . . . We put in a long and nerve wracking [*sic*] afternoon getting ready for an attack believed coming in early evening." About midnight "came the faint notes of a cavalry bugle. No sound was ever more beautiful and the relief almost too great."[1]

The Anglos were so certain they were about to be attacked that, in order to prevent the Kiowas and his Comanches from being associated with a planned attack, Quanah Parker took a few of his headmen to the Chiricahua villages and made a hard threat: "If you'd like to start trouble, we'll take care of you."

The bugle Grace Paulding heard was from soldiers returning from the Rush Springs train station thirty miles away. Lieutenant Beach had sent a report to Fort Sill commandant Edgar R. Kellogg before Kellogg's detachment had left the station, explaining that there seemed to be a strong possibility of a Chiricahua uprising. Soldiers rushed back to stop the attack but found all was quiet at Fort Sill.

When told of the soldiers' return and why they came back, Geronimo jeered at the news and said some ignorant Apache must have started the rumor that the Apaches were all going to have another uprising and massacre the women and children at the fort. Jason Betzinez, who had ridden with Geronimo as a teenager and had just returned from Carlisle after working in a Pennsylvania steel mill, said Geronimo was very disturbed by the story because he was an American soldier and was wearing the uniform. Most of the Chiricahua men at Fort Sill were in fact "in uniform" and felt the same as Geronimo when they learned of the big panic.[2]

Subsequent investigation showed the Apaches had never considered breaking out, that they were peacefully minding their business, and that discipline among them was excellent. The scare had been based totally on rumor and innuendo and, according to Lieutenant Beach, a misinterpretation of the Apache belief that sometime in the future a general conflict with the Anglos would lead to white extermination and the Apaches' reclaiming land from which they had been driven. After the rumors were put to rest, the Apaches continued with their daily lives, the Fort Sill commandant took his detachment to Cuba, and a red-faced Lieutenant Beach wrote his report.

Geronimo Escapes!

Geronimo had broken out of the San Carlos reservation, leaving death and destruction scattered over the southwestern United States and northern Mexico and then surrendered three times in a little more than six years. As a result, over the years of Geronimo's captivity, newspapers waited in eager expectation for news of his next breakout and army chase, events that would sell lots of papers. In at least two major instances, reporters believed Geronimo had escaped and reported it in sensational headlines that soon proved to be false.

In the years the Chiricahuas spent at forts in Florida and Alabama, there was little opportunity for the prisoners to escape. Fort Pickens in Florida, where the bands of Geronimo and Mangas were held, was on Santa Rosa Island surrounded by wide stretches of water, and swamps surrounded Mount Vernon Barracks in Alabama, making an escape with families virtually impossible. Guards at both locations were minimal, and the Apaches had relatively free movement about the camps. When the Chiricahuas were sent to Fort Sill, they had unimpeded access to hundreds of miles of prairie leading back to their old roaming lands in New Mexico and Arizona. Their temptation to leave was great, but they knew Captain Scott, the first commander of the Apache prisoners at Fort Sill, had a map of the trails and waterholes west and was prepared to give chase with Comanches and Kiowas supporting him if they left. However, as the big fairs, expositions, and parades began to ask for Geronimo's attendance, the possibilities for his escape grew far beyond what they might have been at Fort Sill.

The Trans-Mississippi and International Exposition held at Omaha from September 9 through October 30, 1898, was Geronimo's first

Warren Mac Oliver photograph of Geronimo ca. 1907.
COURTESY OF LIBRARY OF CONGRESS

attendance at a major exposition. Selected Fort Sill Chiricahuas, such as Naiche and his family, accompanied him.

On Sundays Geronimo, Naiche, and other Apaches had free time. They got Jimmie Stevens, who was in charge of the San Carlos Apaches at the exposition, to hire a livery team and drive them around so they could see the countryside. One cloudy Sunday, Stevens drove them out across the checkerboard of roads on the pool-table-flat land running between farms and fields of tall corn, and they stopped occasionally to visit with the farm families. The Apaches and Jimmie Stevens became lost. Geronimo later said, "No mountains, nothing but corn." They were supposed to return before dark, but night came and clouds screened the stars they would normally use to guide them. The Apaches' disappearance into the unending sections covered with tall corn and not returning when night came made it appear they were headed for their mountains in Arizona. Omaha was alerted; farmers barred their doors and loaded shotguns; telegraph wires hummed with the news that Geronimo and his Apaches had vanished. Stevens finally found a telephone and called the army officer in charge of the Apaches. He came out and guided them back. They were over twenty miles from Omaha, and it was probably the only time in Geronimo's long life that he was lost.[1]

When the lost wagon carrying Geronimo and others was led back into Omaha, boys on the street were selling extra-edition newspapers with blaring headlines:

Geronimo and Naiche Escape
Apache Murderers Thought to Be on Their Way Back to Arizona

Jimmie Stevens bought a paper and, standing under a streetlight, read the story to the Apaches, after which he didn't waste any time getting them back to their camp.

Nine years later in 1907, Geronimo led the Fourth of July parade in Cache, Oklahoma, riding his best pony, which often won races. Leaving Cache in the late afternoon, Geronimo disappeared. He had apparently started back east to Fort Sill but turned south and hid in the timber along a creek. It's likely that he'd had a little too much to drink. However, it was widely reported that he was headed to Mexico to join the Apaches who still had camps in the Sierra Madre. Soldiers found him the next day and escorted him back to Fort Sill. So ended another scare story of Apaches breaking away from their captivity when nothing ever happened.[2]

Geronimo, Superstar

GERONIMO WAS IN HIS EARLY SIXTIES WHEN HE SURRENDERED TO GENeral Miles in 1886. When Gen. D. S. Stanley, army commander at San Antonio, a few weeks later made a written record listing and describing the members of Geronimo's band at the request of President Grover Cleveland, he guessed Geronimo's age to be forty-seven. Geronimo spent the remaining twenty-three years of his life in captivity as a prisoner of war, but with his vigor, drive, and reputation, he became one of the best-known and most popular Indians in the United States.

Contrary to then popular belief, Geronimo was very rarely behind bars during his captivity. He claimed that he was in the Fort Sill guardhouse only twice and only for two or three days to sleep off drunks from bootleg whiskey. Geronimo's first exposure to crowds began when he and his little band were shipped east. When the train carrying them stopped for water and wood or coal, they were often let off to stretch and be seen by the locals, who wanted to see the "raiders and murderers."

They were held in San Antonio for six weeks while President Cleveland made up his mind about what to do with them after discovering General Miles's obfuscation in what he had said were the terms of surrender. Crowds from San Antonio came to look over the prisoners at the fort, where a photograph was taken of a despondent Geronimo leaning against a quadrangle wall. He thought they were all about to be executed.[1]

President Cleveland determined the federal government was responsible for the Naiche-Geronimo band and sent them on to Florida. The women and children were sent to Fort Marion in Saint Augustine, and Geronimo and his warriors went to Fort Pickens on Santa Rosa Island in Pensacola Bay. At both forts, tourists came to ogle the prisoners. The

Photos of Geronimo, L–R starting at top: Judge at Mount Vernon, at the 1904 Saint Louis Louisiana Purchase Exposition, in Theodore Roosevelt's inaugural parade in 1905 (second from the right on the dark horse in the row of chiefs), driving the Locomobile at the 101 Ranch in 1905, and in headdresses at Fort Sill ca. 1904, 1906, and 1907.
COURTESY OF NATIONAL ARCHIVES AND LIBRARY OF CONGRESS

Chiricahuas at Fort Marion were soon selling personal items and souvenirs to make enough money to buy food after the army quartermaster determined they didn't need full rations. At Fort Pickens, because visitors first had to get a pass from the fort commander and then travel by boat to Santa Rosa Island, tourist traffic was initially slow but gradually picked up until there were rarely fewer than 20 a day, and one day the tourist count reached 457.

After their women and children were returned to them in late April 1887, the prisoners on Santa Rosa Island soon learned that, with Wratten to help them communicate with the tourists, they, too, could make money selling souvenirs. Geronimo made bow and arrows, and after Wratten showed him how to write his name, he made extra money selling his autograph. At Fort Pickens, Geronimo began to understand how Anglo commercialism worked, and he learned his lessons well.

After a year and a half on Santa Rosa Island, the Naiche-Geronimo band, Mangas, and the young warrior Goso were transferred to Mount Vernon Barracks in the piney woods and swamps thirty miles north of Mobile, Alabama. For a while, the only souvenir sales for the Apaches were at the stores in the little town of Mount Vernon. However, the Chiricahuas learned passengers on the trains stopping at Mount Vernon Station were a good source of revenue. The tourists wanted anything Geronimo made, and as a result he was selling items such as bow and arrows for the other men, never telling the tourists they weren't actually his. One visitor noted that the things the Apaches offered for sale were "very handsome and ingenious" and that Geronimo was very active in the business. The visitor bought a signed headdress and large bead necklace from Geronimo, after dickering down the asking price of $25. If he bought it for half the asking price (as is common today at stores selling Indian crafts), Geronimo would have made about $345 in today's coin.

The army sent the Chiricahuas to live at Fort Sill in early October 1894. Even then, eight years after his surrender, crowds gathered at the train stops from Mobile to New Orleans to Fort Worth to applaud and curse Geronimo. Within a year after they arrived, the Apaches had souvenirs available for sale in the trading post Wratten managed, but sales came mainly from soldiers and the few visitors to the post. After the town of nearby Lawton was established in 1901, the Chiricahua souvenir business increased significantly.

In 1898, Geronimo and others were invited to participate in their first exposition, the Trans-Mississippi and International Exposition held in Omaha from September 9 to October 30, 1898. At crowded stops along the way, Geronimo sold buttons off his coat for twenty-five cents, and the hat he wore sold for five dollars. Once the train started moving again, he sewed on more buttons and pulled another hat out of his box of hats to sell at the next stop.

In Omaha, after twelve years of captivity in three different locations, Geronimo came face-to-face with General Miles, who had promised forgiveness for "bad things" Geronimo and his warriors had done, reunion with their families in five days, two years of exile in Florida, and then their own reservation on good land. (The idea of two years of exile in Florida actually came from Gen. George Crook when Geronimo first surrendered in March 1886, but Miles didn't disabuse Geronimo of the promise.) A public debate was set up between Geronimo and Miles, and a large crowd gathered to watch the confrontation. Jimmie Stevens served as interpreter.[2]

Stevens's father had owned sheep and Jimmie an expensive pony that Geronimo had killed and eaten at the 1882 Ash Flat Massacre, when nine Mexican sheepherders, their wives and children, and a Mexican foreman, who as a child Geronimo had kidnapped and raised for a while, were killed. Stevens said he wanted fifty dollars for his pony, but decided he'd settle for seeing Geronimo embarrassed. As Angie Debo notes, the killing of the Mexicans that day didn't seem to matter to Jimmie.[2] Geronimo accused Miles of lying about his promises. Miles smiled and said that yes he had lied, but he had learned lying "from the greatest nantan of all liars—from you, Geronimo. You lied to Mexicans, Americans, and to your own Apaches for thirty years. White men only lied to you once, and I did it." Geronimo then made a case for the Chiricahuas to be returned to Arizona, but Miles mocked him and said no.

Other exposition developers saw the crowds Geronimo had drawn in Omaha. He was invited to the Pan-American Exposition at Buffalo, New York, from May to October 1901, where he was paid forty-five dollars a month and sold his souvenirs. But the exposition didn't draw much attention until President William McKinley was shot there on September 6. Soon Pawnee Bill's Wild West Show requested that Geronimo participate in a seven-month tour, to which he agreed, if the War Department approved. There were also requests from other commercial shows, and all were turned down by the War Department. However, the request generated much more publicity than the refusal, leading to the frequent statement that Geronimo traveled with Pawnee Bill's show.

As long as Geronimo stayed in Oklahoma, requests for his appearance required only his approval and that of the post commander. He began appearing at celebrations throughout the territory; he rode in a Fourth of

July parade at nearby Lawton in 1902, later that fall in a big Oklahoma City parade, and in the 1903 Fourth of July parade in Anadarko.

In 1904, Geronimo went to the Louisiana Purchase Exposition in Saint Louis.[3, 4] There, he was reunited with Lenna, his daughter by Ih-tedda, the Mescalero wife he had divorced. He hadn't seen Lenna since she was a baby. Now she was a beautiful seventeen-year-old, and both were delighted by the reunion.[5]

Geronimo and five chiefs from the Plains Wars were invited to ride in Theodore Roosevelt's inaugural parade. Crowds of spectators left their expensive seats on Pennsylvania Avenue to follow Geronimo and cheer him on. Woodworth Clum, son of John Clum, the former Indian agent at San Carlos and the only man ever actually to capture Geronimo, said with disgust that you would think Geronimo was "Public Hero No. 2" based on all the cheers he drew. A few days later, Geronimo asked Roosevelt to let him return to his own country, but Roosevelt refused, fearing major bloodshed caused by Arizona settlers wanting to settle old scores.

At all the events he attended, Geronimo sold his souvenirs—bows and arrows, canes, quivers, and autographed photographs. His popularity across the land made him the equivalent of a modern-day superstar. When he passed away, he left a small fortune in a Lawton bank account, and virtually all the Apaches and most white people from Lawton and soldiers at Fort Sill attended his funeral. He dreamed often of returning to his own country, but it was a dream unfulfilled. He died and was buried on the prairie in Oklahoma, a prisoner of war.

Geronimo at the Saint Louis
Louisiana Purchase Exposition

THE LOUISIANA PURCHASE EXPOSITION (OR WORLD'S FAIR) WAS HELD at Saint Louis in 1904. Congress appropriated $40,000 plus a supplemental $25,000 for the Department of Interior to show original Indian culture and how Indians were being educated. S. M. McCowan, the superintendent at the Indian boarding school in Chilocco, Oklahoma, was placed in charge of the exhibit.

When promoters learned that "wild" Indians, perhaps including Chiricahua Apaches with Geronimo, would be at the exposition, they pushed for Wild West shows to be set up on the midway and asked that the Indians participating in the cultural exhibit do reenactments of the old days. However, Washington officials stopped that foolishness, even though Pawnee Bill tried several times to get War Department approval for Geronimo to tour with his Wild West show. The War Department refused every commercial request, drawing a clear line between commercial exhibitions and official celebrations when it came to the exploitation of its Indian prisoners.

Geronimo was never permitted to participate in the commercial touring exhibitions. Captain Farrand Sayre, commander of the Fort Sill prisoners, required that Geronimo attend under McGowan's supervision. Sayre's plan for the Saint Louis exhibition was to send nine Chiricahuas, including Geronimo, with George Wratten, who would help them get set up and settled and then return to Fort Sill. The Chiricahuas were to earn about a dollar a day plus money they made selling their souvenirs. They were set to leave on May 10, 1904, but a promoter got to Geronimo with

Gerhard Sisters photograph of Geronimo at the 1904 Saint Louis Louisiana Purchase Exposition.
COURTESY OF NATIONAL ARCHIVES

an offer of one hundred dollars a month (he had made forty-five dollars
a month at the Buffalo exposition in 1901). On May 9, Geronimo told
Captain Sayre he wanted more money, or he wouldn't go. The others left
without him. Within about two weeks, Geronimo concluded that he
could attend the exposition only on the War Department's terms, and he

told Captain Sayre that he had been badly advised and was willing to go even without pay. He sounded like a classic politician in the autobiography he dictated to S. M. Barrett when he said, "When I was first asked to attend the St. Louis World's Fair, I did not wish to go. Later, when I was told that I would receive good attention and protection, and that the President of the United States said it would be all right, I consented."[1]

Arriving at the fair, Geronimo lived in the Apache Village near the Indian Building. Each represented tribe lived in village lodges that were typical of the tribe. In the Indian Building, he had a booth where he worked on his bows and arrows and sold his autograph and photographs. McGowan even got orders for Geronimo's pictures and other merchandise in the mail. Geronimo got ten, fifteen, or twenty-five cents for an autograph, twenty-five cents for a photograph (of which he kept ten cents since the government was supplying the photographs), and several dollars for a signed bow and arrow.

Thomas Dahkeya, Geronimo's grandson, then about fourteen, attended the fair with him and earned his keep doing day-to-day chores and helping out at the booth (probably as an interpreter) where Geronimo worked. Around the middle of July, Geronimo was delighted to meet Lenna, his beautiful teenaged daughter by Ih-tedda. Lenna had come to represent the Mescaleros, but she had eye trachoma so bad she couldn't work. She stayed with Geronimo and Thomas in their tipi for over a month.

As they visited and talked, Lenna told him her mother had a son seven months after she returned to Mescalero. Lenna's story was the first clue Geronimo had that he might have a son of whom he had not been aware. Ih-tedda had named her son Robert but claimed the boy's father was Old Cross Eyes, the scout her father had forced her to marry a few days after she returned. Ih-tedda later admitted that Geronimo was the boy's father. Geronimo came to know Robert when the boy began attending school in Chilocco that fall, and he declared the boy was his son.[2, 3] Thereafter, Geronimo stayed in close contact with Lenna and followed what went on with Ih-tedda's family.

While at the exposition, Geronimo attended shows and tried out the rides on the midway. It was an interesting experience. He saw "strange men [Turks] with red caps and peculiar swords" they used in staged battles. After watching a mock fight, he decided, "They would be hard people to kill in a hand-to-hand fight." He saw "little brown people," Igorots, from the Philippines. He said of the Igorots, "They didn't wear much clothing, and I think they should not have been allowed to come to the fair. But they themselves did not seem to know any better."

Geronimo believed the magic shows he saw were demonstrations of supernatural power. He saw a woman put in a basket that was covered with a cloth and run through with swords. He was certain she was dead until the cloth was lifted and she walked out smiling. At another show, a black man tied with a rope managed to slip free with the knots still in place. Geronimo said, "I do not understand how this was done. It was certainly a miraculous power because no man could have released himself by his own efforts."

Geronimo saw puppets, strange little people, who "did not seem in earnest about anything they did; so I only laughed at them. All the people around where we sat seemed to be laughing at me." He saw a trained bear and, not believing bears to be very intelligent, was surprised to see this one do whatever it was told. He said, "I'm sure no grizzly bear could be trained to do those things."[2]

He rode a Ferris wheel and, looking out the window, was surprised to see houses appearing to go up and down, apparently not realizing the car in which he rode was attached to a great turning wheel. Making objects from glass fascinated him. He had always thought glass objects were made by hand but was surprised to see a glassblower do his magic with the amorphous clear blob on the end of his blowpipe. He said, "I bought many curious things and brought them home with me." Most were probably for Eva, who was looking after a very fragile Zi-yeh.

He summed up his trip saying, "I am glad I went to the fair. I saw many interesting things and learned much of the white people. . . . I wish all my people could have attended the Fair. . . . I sold my photographs at a profit and wrote my name for a price and kept all that money. I often made as much as two dollars a day, and when I returned I had plenty of money—more than I had ever earned before."

McCowan had been irked by Geronimo's refusal to attend the fair because he wasn't paid enough and had written to Captain Sayre, "You and I agree fully that Geronimo is not more than a blatant blackguard, living on a false reputation." By the end of the exposition, McGowan, changing his mind, wrote Sayre, "He [Geronimo] really has endeared himself to whites and Indians alike. With one or two exceptions, when he was not feeling well, he was gentle, kind, and courteous. I did not think I could ever speak so kindly of the old fellow whom I have always regarded as an incarnate fiend. I am very glad to return him to you in as sound and healthy condition as when you brought him here."[2]

Geronimo's Contemporaries:
The Great Chiefs

IN 1905, GERONIMO RODE IN THEODORE ROOSEVELT'S INAUGURAL parade with five other well-known chiefs and war leaders: Little Plume, Piegan Blackfoot; Buckskin Charlie, Southern Ute; Quanah Parker, Comanche; Hollow Horn Bear, Brulé Sioux; and American Horse, Oglala Sioux. At the time of the parade, Quanah Parker was about sixty; American Horse, about sixty-five. Little Plume's age is unknown, but he was probably no more than seventy. Hollow Horn Bear was about fifty-five; Buckskin Charlie, about sixty-five; and Geronimo, about eighty. Geronimo, the old man of the group, rode wrapped in his blanket, calm and self-assured, and that day he was second only to the president in terms of popularity.

After the parade, Roosevelt is said to have told his advisors he hoped he never heard Geronimo's name again. Quanah Parker and the Sioux chiefs were Plains Indian warriors. The Ute and Blackfoot warriors appeared on the plains but were better known for life in and around the Rocky Mountains. When Geronimo was captured for the first and only time by San Carlos agent John Clum and his tribal police and driven shakled to the San Carlos guardhouse in 1877, Sitting Bull, Crazy Horse, and the Sioux and Cheyenne chiefs had wiped out Gen. Armstrong Custer a year earlier. Also a little earlier (beginning in 1875), Quanah Parker had surrendered to Bad Hand (Col. Ranald S. Mackenzie) and settled on the Comanche-Kiowa reservation in southwestern Oklahoma under Agent James M. Hayworth.[1, 2]

For 150 years, the Apaches west of the Pecos River and the Comanches had been blood enemies. Despite that fact, they were still willing

Geronimo with the great chiefs and warriors who rode in Theodore Roosevelt's 1905 inaugural parade, L–R: Little Plume, Piegan Blackfoot; Buckskin Charlie, Southern Ute; Geronimo, Chiricahua Apache; Quanah Parker, Comanche; Hollow Horn Bear, Brulé Sioux; and American Horse, Oglala Sioux.
COURTESY OF NATIONAL ARCHIVES

to call truces in order to fight the hated White Eyes. Quanah Parker became chief of the Comanches on their reservation, and when the Chiricahua Apaches were sent to Fort Sill about twenty years later, Quanah Parker and many other Comanches and Kiowas were there to meet them and were willing to share their reservation lands. Geronimo learned to speak Comanche well and became a personal friend of Quanah Parker.

In the early years before the reservations, Mangas Coloradas, the great Mimbreño chief, war leader, and organizer of the Apache bands, began a war with Mexico after the 1837 Santa Rita copper mines massacre, when the great Apache chief Juan José Compa and others were killed for their scalps. Later, in the 1850s, during Mangas Coloradas's war with the Americans, Geronimo and Victorio became major war leaders and, at times, individually led as many as fifty warriors on deadly raids into Mexico. After Geronimo's entire family was wiped out around 1850, Mangas Coloradas gave him the honor of leading all the Apaches whose families the Mexican soldiers had attacked and killed the year before. The battle wiped out the Mexican soldiers who had attacked the camp of Mangas but cost the lives of many warriors.[3]

In January 1861, Cochise escaped Lt. George N. Bascom in the "cut through the tent" affair to wage war on the Americans for the next eleven years. In 1872, Cochise signed a treaty with General Howard after getting the agent (Tom Jeffords) and reservation land in the Dragoon and Chiricahua Mountains that he wanted. He let Geronimo and his brother-in-law, the great Nednhi chief Juh, settle on a piece of the reservation land with a boundary on part of the Mexican border, allowing them easy access to Mexico for war and raids without having to bypass American soldiers guarding the border. Juh, who preferred his stronghold camps in the Sierra Madre to those on reservation land and was not as well known to the American press as Geronimo, was probably the strongest war leader the Apaches had from about 1871 until he died (likely from a stroke or heart attack) in the fall of 1883.

Chokonen Chiricahua chief Taza (Cochise's elder son), whom Cochise had groomed to take his place, unexpectedly died only two years after Cochise had gone to the Happy Place. Cochise's youngest son, Naiche, then became chief at nineteen. Naiche didn't have the maturity, leadership skills, or supernatural power from Ussen to be the chief his people needed. About 1880, Geronimo became Naiche's counselor. Naiche gave his authority to be war leader to Geronimo, who had great war-making power.

Chihuahua was chief of a sub-band of Chokonen Chiricahuas and was a protégé of Cochise. He and his older brother Ulzana, his segundo, who was famous for a raid across New Mexico and Arizona in 1885, fought in and supported Cochise's war with the Anglos. When Cochise went to his reservation, Chihuahua and Ulzana took their people to San Carlos. They didn't accept Cochise's sons as chiefs, but they were not involved in the battle that attempted to remove Taza and Naiche in 1876. When Geronimo broke out of San Carlos in September 1881 and headed for the Sierra Madre Mountains in Mexico, Chihuahua went too. He surrendered, along with all the other Apache leaders and chiefs, to General Crook in 1883 and returned to San Carlos. He broke out again in 1885 with Geronimo but surrendered to General Crook in March 1886 (the same time as Geronimo, who then changed his mind and didn't surrender to General Miles until September 4, 1886) and was shipped with his people to Fort Marion in Saint Augustine, Florida, on April 7, 1886.

After the army murdered Mangas Coloradas in early 1863, the leading chiefs of the Mimbreño Apaches became Victorio and Loco. Nana was Victorio's segundo and son-in-law. After Mexican soldiers wiped out Victorio at Tres Castillos in the fall of 1880, Nana became the leader of Victorio's people, with Kaytennae as his segundo. Then Nana died in 1896, and Kaytennae assumed band leadership. In August 1881, Nana, probably over eighty and so crippled by arthritis that he could barely walk, led a six-week revenge raid that left a trail of death and destruction wherever it went. He then disappeared into Mexico and was not seen again until he, along with Geronimo and other leaders living in the Sierra Madre, surrendered to General Crook and returned to Fort Apache in 1883. Nana later broke out of San Carlos with Geronimo in 1885.

Loco and his people had made peace with the Americans and lived quietly on the San Carlos reservation until Geronimo, Nana, and others, after escaping to the Sierra Madre and needing more warriors to fight Mexican soldiers, decided to "rescue" the Loco people from San Carlos in 1882. The Loco people were forced at gunpoint to leave San Carlos and run for the Apache camps in the Sierra Madre.

Eskiminzin was chief of the Aravaipa Apaches and suffered many injustices at the hands of the Anglos. Because his daughter had married Apache Kid, the army accused Eskiminzin of supporting Kid with bullets and other supplies. Eskiminzin claimed he was innocent, but he was sent to Mount Vernon Barracks with about forty of his people, where they suffered in the swamps with Geronimo and the Chiricahuas. When the Chiricahuas were sent to Fort Sill, Eskiminzin and his people were returned to San Carlos. No doubt during the time they were together at Mount Vernon, the two old warriors came to know each other well.[4]

About three months after President Roosevelt's parade, Geronimo was invited to attend a big exhibition at the 101 Ranch for newspaper managers. A photograph shows him riding in the Locomobile with Ponca chief Edward Leclair. Geronimo so admired Leclair's beaded vest that at the end of the day, Leclair gave it to him. When Geronimo died four years later, he was buried with his most treasured possessions and was said to have been wearing Leclair's beaded vest.

It is remarkable to look across the life of Geronimo and see the great chiefs and war leaders with whom he was associated in friendship or in war. He was a major war leader for Mangas Coloradas and led big raids into Mexico along with Victorio. He knew Victorio's segundo, Nana (who was married to Geronimo's sister); Nana's segundo, Kaytennae; and the great but generally peaceable warrior Loco. His brother-in-law Juh, with whom he made many raids and fought many battles, was the greatest Apache war chief in Mexico. He was counselor to Cochise's son, knew Cochise's protégé, Chihuahua, well, and served time at Mount Vernon with the Aravaipa chief Eskiminzin. In his later years as a captive, he became friends with the great Comanche chief Quanah Parker, and he knew warrior chiefs from the Great Plains and the Rocky Mountains: American Horse, Little Plume, Hollow Horn Bear, Buckskin Charlie, and Edward Leclair. Truly Geronimo was known by and knew the great warriors of his time who fought against the tsunami of Anglos and Mexicans sweeping over them. They did not go quietly into the dark night.

Geronimo's Children

FOLLOWING APACHE BLOODLINES IS COMPLICATED. FOR EXAMPLE, before and well into reservation times, Apaches sometimes had more than one wife (a man could take as many wives as he could support), and often, as was common with the Mescaleros, the wives were sisters. Hence, if a child's father had two or three wives, the child might have full-blooded brothers or sisters from the same mother or half brothers or sisters from another wife, all of which were referred to as "brother" or "sister," regardless of who the child's mother was. However, when the half brothers or sisters married, their children would call each other brother or sister, whereas white society would call them cousins. Thus, Geronimo's

Geronimo's surviving children with his divorced wife, Ih-tedda, L–R: Lenna about age seventeen; Ih-tedda with Lenna, about age three, to her right and holding Robert, about age one; and Robert, about age fifty-three in 1942.
COURTESY OF NATIONAL ARCHIVES AND THE LYNDA SÁNCHEZ/EVE BALL COLLECTION

father, Taklishim, had a half sister, who would have been Geronimo's aunt in white parlance. She had a girl child, Ishton, who would have been, in white parlance, Geronimo's cousin.[1] Geronimo dearly loved her and referred to her as his sister. Ishton married the Nednhi chief Juh. Geronimo referred to Juh as his brother-in-law and Ishton's first child Daklugie, who she nearly died delivering, as his nephew, and Daklugie thought of Geronimo as his uncle. In the white way of counting relations, Daklugie would have been Geronimo's second cousin. Daklugie's children would have been Geronimo's third cousins. A child of Geronimo would have been a fourth cousin to a child of Daklugie.

In the United States, it's legal for second cousins to marry. However, when Geronimo's surviving son, Robert Geronimo, married his fourth cousin, Maude Daklugie (they were then both past fifty), Daklugie, who liked Robert, still made them divorce because he believed they were too closely related. Incest is the worst kind of crime for Apaches, and knowingly committing incest was considered dead certain proof the person who did it was a witch who should be burned. Daklugie believed Ishton was Geronimo's sister and that therefore Robert and Maude were first cousins and too closely related to marry.[2]

There are many who claim to be descendants of Geronimo, and they may well have some distant cousin relationship, but as demonstrated above, it's difficult to establish a direct descent bloodline despite references by an elderly family member referring to brothers or sisters. The question therefore arises as to who the known children of Geronimo were and from whom descent might be claimed.

Geronimo's first wife was Alope. They had three children, who, along with Alope and Geronimo's mother, were all killed by the Mexican army from Sonora around 1850, as Geronimo said, at the time of the United States–Mexico border survey. The oldest child was under ten, and their names are not known. Apache custom requires that given Apache names not be repeated after death.

Geronimo's second wife was Chee-hash-kish. It is known that Chee-hash-kish had a son and daughter. The son, Chappo, born in about 1862 or 1863, was a scout in Company B at Fort Apache in 1884 and left the reservation with Geronimo in May 1885. He surrendered with

Geronimo in 1886 and was sent to the Carlisle Indian school in 1888. Six years later, Chappo was sent back to his family at Mount Vernon Barracks, Alabama, where he died in September 1894; his wife, Nahd-clohnn, and their baby passed away at about the same time. Chee-hash-kish's daughter, Dohn-say (aka Tozey and known at Fort Sill as Lulu), was born in about 1866 or 1865. Chee-hash-kish was captured by the Mexicans in 1882 near Casas Grandes and sold into slavery. Geronimo never saw her again, although he made a number of inquiries and stole some Mexican women to trade for her. But his attempts at her rescue proved futile for one reason or another.[3]

There is a belief in Mexico that Chee-hash-kish had two more children in the 1860s, a girl, Victoriana, and a boy, Casimir, and that Geronimo deliberately avoided any reference to them so they could safely hide in Mexico with their mother, who had been saved from slavery by a murky white renegade figure named Zebina Streeter. However, it's hard to believe that an Apache woman, especially one on the run during wartime, would have four children in the space of six or seven years when Apaches normally spaced their children about four years apart. Furthermore, Chiricahua friends or enemies of Geronimo never mentioned these children.

In 1872, Geronimo and Juh settled on the back part of the Cochise reservation next to the Mexican border, where they could raid south whenever they wanted without army interference. During this time, Geronimo took a woman, Nana-tha-thtith, who was closely related to Cochise. Nana-tha-thtith and her child were killed by Mexican troops two or three years later.

American troops under Capt. Wirt Davis captured Geronimo's daughter, Dohn-say, in early August 1885. Dohn-say was in captivity with Geronimo and married a warrior, Mike Dahkeya, who had surrendered with Chihuahua. Dahkeya and Dohn-say had three children: Thomas, Nina, and Joe. Dohn-say died in 1898. Her last surviving child, Geronimo's grandson Thomas, for whom Geronimo had high hopes in carrying on his family line, died at age eighteen in March 1908, eleven months before his grandfather passed away.

By 1885, Geronimo had married three other women. They were Zi-yeh, She-gha, and Shtsha-she. When in August 1885 Captain Davis took Geronimo's camp in the mountains northeast of Nacorí, Mexico (the same raid in which Dohn-say was taken), it was reported that three wives and five children of Geronimo's family were captured. It is known that Zi-yeh and She-gha were among them. If there was, in fact, a third wife, then it must have been Shtsha-she, but she soon vanished and does not appear in any other accounts of Geronimo's family. By this time, Geronimo's daughter Dohn-say would have been close to twenty. It's possible the army mistook her for Geronimo wife. It's certainly not likely she would have been counted as a child. At that time, Zi-yeh had a young son about four, Fenton; there was a three-year-old girl whose identity has not been established; and there was a two-year-old boy whose mother is unknown and who died after the group reached Fort Bowie. He is buried in the post cemetery with the name Little Robe. Nothing is known of the remaining two children.

In late September 1885, Geronimo and four of his warriors slipped back across the border to try to retake their wives. Geronimo was able to get back She-gha but not Zi-yeh. On the way back to Mexico, Geronimo and his followers were able to kidnap some Mescalero women and children who were on leave from the Mescalero reservation and collecting a big piñon nut harvest in southwestern New Mexico. Geronimo took a young Mescalero woman, Ih-tedda (young girl), and made her his wife.

On January 16, 1886, Lt. Marion Maus met with Geronimo and his leading warriors to discuss a possible surrender to General Crook. Geronimo agreed to meet with Crook to "talk about surrendering in two moons." As a show of good faith, Geronimo gave Lieutenant Maus nine "prisoners" (hostages) to hold until the talks were over. Among the hostages was his wife Ih-tedda, newly pregnant with her first child—even then Geronimo was looking after her—and his wife Zi-yeh and child Fenton, then four or five years old.

Geronimo broke away two days after agreeing to surrender to General Crook in March 1886. The army then shipped all the remaining Chiricahuas who had surrendered plus most of the hostages (a total of seventy-seven) to Fort Marion in Florida.

Ih-tedda had her baby, the only Indian child born that month at Fort Marion in September 1886. The post commander, Lt. Col. Loomis L.

Langdon, recorded the baby's name as Marion, but she somehow acquired the name Lenna, by which she was known for the rest of her life. Geronimo now had three children (Dohn-say, Fenton, and Lenna) and two wives (Ih-tedda and Zi-yeh) at Fort Marion. Geronimo's third wife, She-gha, who had run with him after the March meeting, was sent on to Fort Marion after Geronimo was left at Fort Pickens. Eight months after Lenna was born, in April 1887, the army moved the prisoners at Fort Marion to Mount Vernon Barracks in Alabama, where there was more room but living conditions were actually worse. On the way, the families of the Fort Pickens prisoners were left at Fort Pickens to be reunited with their men. The band at Fort Pickens was sent to Mount Vernon Barracks to be reunited with the other Chiricahuas a year later in May 1888.

After the army agreed to let the Mescaleros return to their reservation, Geronimo divorced Ih-tedda, even with her begging him to let her stay, so she and his daughter could escape the prison camp. Unknown to Geronimo, Ih-tedda was pregnant with their second child, but when the boy was born in August of that year, he was given the name of Ih-tedda's second husband and called Robert Cross Eyes.

Eight or nine months after Ih-tedda went back to Mescalero in 1889, Zi-yeh had Geronimo's last child, Eva, a little girl on whom he doted. He depended on her greatly in her mid-teenage years to help him with her dying mother. After Geronimo died in 1909, Eva married a few months later, apparently against Geronimo's wishes, and in 1910 gave birth to a daughter who lived barely two months. Eva died in 1911, probably from tuberculosis.

At the Saint Louis Louisiana Purchase Exposition in 1904, Geronimo again met his beautiful seventeen-year-old daughter Lenna after fifteen years of separation. Surprisingly, when he dictated his autobiography to S. M. Barrett the next year, he didn't mention his reunion with Lenna, but the details of the Mescalero family must have come from what he learned from her, including the fact that Ih-tedda's son Robert might very well be his child. It's also clear he kept in touch with her because he knew of her subsequent marriage.[4] Geronimo and Robert first met at Chilocco in 1906, and Geronimo was convinced the boy was his son.

When Geronimo died in February 1909, Eva and Robert were in school at Chilocco. After the funeral, Eva completed the term at Chilocco and then married a fellow student. Robert stayed at Fort Sill and eventually went to school at Carlisle, from which he was discharged on June 7, 1916. He settled in Mescalero and married Esta Rodriguez, Mescalero Lipan Apache. They had three daughters: Martha, Ouida, and a third child, who died in infancy, Betsie Liberty Geronimo. Robert married Juanita Rodriguez, Esta's sister, after Esta passed away. They had three children: Robert Jr., Larry, and Eva Ann Geronimo. After Juanita passed away, he married a third wife, Maude Daklugie, but they divorced without children at Daklugie's insistence because Daklugie believed they were too closely related (in fact they were fourth cousins and not too closely related).[2]

Robert was one of the most successful stockmen on the reservation and was president of the Mescalero Cattle Growers Association around 1938. He died in October 1966 and was buried at Mescalero.

Sometime after 1905, Lenna married Juan Via, a Lipan Apache. They had four children: Ella, Annie, Juanito, and Percy Via. Lenna died in 1919, and Ella died at age thirteen in 1920, both deaths probably resulting from the lingering effects of the 1918 flu epidemic. Annie, Juanito, and Percy survived, along with Robert's children, to carry on Geronimo's direct line, with descendants now still living in Mescalero.

Eve Ball, author of *Indeh*, interviewed Ih-tedda (Katie Cross Eyes) in the hospital in around 1950 using an Apache nurse to interpret Ih-tedda's words for her into English. Ih-tedda's story to Eve is that told in the book *Indeh*.[5]

Of all the wives and their children who can be reliably traced or were known by the Chiricahuas to have lived, only the children of Ih-tedda, Lenna and Robert, survived to have children of their own who carried on Geronimo's direct line. Many of their children, grandchildren, and generations beyond continue Geronimo's bloodline at Mescalero. Geronimo did a noble thing by forcing his wife to leave him in order to save her life and that of his daughter. He was rewarded with a bloodline that continues to this day.

Eva Geronimo

By divorcing his Mescalero wife, Ih-tedda, Geronimo was left with only one wife at Mount Vernon Barracks, the diminutive Zi-yeh, mother of his seven- or eight-year-old son Fenton. On September 23, 1889, eight months after Ih-tedda and little daughter Lenna left Mount Vernon, Zi-yeh gave birth to Eva, Geronimo's last child, to whom he was devoted.

Zi-yeh apparently was impressed with the faith of the Catholic nuns who worked to help educate the young children at Fort Marion. In July 1890 Zi-yeh and ten-month-old infant daughter Eva were baptized in the Catholic Church at Mount Vernon. Angie Debo suggests this ceremony may be the source of the cross on Geronimo's headdress.[1]

In 1893, an observant visitor at Mount Vernon Barracks who saw the Geronimo family one Sunday when they came to visit him, noted how well Geronimo and Zi-yeh dressed and that, rather than having Zi-yeh carry Eva on a *tsach* (cradleboard) on her back, Geronimo delightedly pulled Eva (then three) in a little express wagon. Others noted that when the crafty businessman Geronimo went into a mercantile store for supplies and Eva happened to be along, whatever the child asked for, her father bought.

In a famous picture taken at Fort Sill, Geronimo stands beside Nina Dahkeya (age three or four), his grandson Thomas (age five), daughter Eva (age six), and Zi-yeh in their pumpkin patch, each holding a pumpkin in his or her arms.[2]

Eldridge Ayer Burbank, who did several paintings of Geronimo, painted Eva at age nine in 1898 and said of her in his notes, "Nobody could be kinder to a child than Geronimo was to her."

Eva about age sixteen on the left, Geronimo, and Emily Chihuahua, Eva's cousin, also about age sixteen, on the right, ca. 1905.

Zi-yeh died of tubercular lupus in 1904. Geronimo then had only Eva living with him, as Fenton had died in 1897 at age sixteen or seventeen. In late summer of 1905, Geronimo gave Eva an elaborate womanhood ceremony, which typically lasted four days. Ramona Chihuahua and probably her sister, Emily, are thought to have helped with the women's part of the ceremony. Geronimo invited all the Apaches, many Kiowas and Comanches, and S. M. Barrett, to whom, with the help of Daklugie as interpreter, he would give his life's story during the following fall and winter. A level place with a large circle of closely mowed grass on Medicine Bluff Creek near Naiche's village was the site of the ceremony. Naiche led the singing, and Geronimo, with the assistance of the medicine men in charge of the ceremony, led the dancing. An all-night celebration closing the ceremony began with a social dance in which the entire group joined hands and danced in a circle around a large fire in the center. When the moon began its descent, the sound of beating drums changed to that of flutes, which was the signal for the older people to withdraw and the "lovers' dance" to begin. In this dance, the young men formed a circle close to the fire, and the young women formed an outer circle. One after the other, the young women danced to the inner circle, and each selected a partner with whom she danced the wheel dance until dawn. At the end of the dance, the young man was expected to give his partner a gift. Such dances often were also the prelude to young men offering women's parents bridal gifts requesting to marry their daughters.[3]

With the rising sun, the dancing stopped, and some betrothals were announced during the giving of gifts. Barrett and Geronimo were among the last to leave, and Geronimo told Barrett that Eva had probably chosen her husband. However, she didn't marry until four years later after Geronimo had passed away. Perhaps Geronimo didn't give his consent, as might be concluded from what he told Daklugie before his death. Daklugie reported that, as Geronimo lay at the edge of death from pneumonia in 1909, he said, "My Nephew, promise me that you and Ramona will take my daughter, Eva, into your home and care for her as you do your own children. Promise me that you won't let her marry. If you do, she will die. The women of our family have great difficulty in childbirth as Ishton [Daklugie's mother] had. Don't let this happen to Eva!" Geronimo dozed off for a little while. When he spoke again, he said, "I want your promise." Daklugie said, "Ramona and I will take your daughter and love her as our own. But how can I prevent her from marrying?" The old man said, "She'll obey you. She has been taught to obey. See that she does." Daklugie said Geronimo died with his fingers clutching his hand.[4]

At the time of Geronimo's death, Eva was in school in Chilocco, Oklahoma, with her half brother Robert. Lieutenant George Purington, in charge of the Apaches at Fort Sill, sent a letter rather than a telegram to Chilocco to tell them of their father's serious illness and that they needed to come. They came as soon as they received the letter, but the funeral services had to be delayed half an hour to allow time for their train to arrive. After the funeral, Eva returned to Chilocco and finished the term, but that was the end of her schooling. She returned to Fort Sill and lived with the Daklugies. Although they tried to talk her out of marrying, as Geronimo had directed when he was dying, she married a fellow student at Chilocco, Fred Godeley. She had a daughter, Evaline, who was born to them on June 21, 1910. The baby lived two months and died on August 20, 1910. Eva died less than a year later, probably from tuberculosis, on August 10, 1911. She was buried between her father and daughter on one side of his grave. Her mother was on the other side and Fenton nearby. Not far away are the graves of her half sister Dohn-say Dahkeya (aka Lulu) and her family. None of the captives who were direct descendants of Geronimo at Fort Sill lived to carry on the family name, and they were buried there with him.

Robert, the Son Geronimo
Didn't Know He Had

ROBERT WAS A BRIGHT CHILD AND WENT TO THE INDIAN SCHOOL AT Chilocco, Oklahoma, in late August 1906 for more advanced training than he could receive at the Mescalero boarding school.[1] About the same time, Geronimo attended his second exhibition at the 101 Ranch operated by the Miller brothers, sons of Col. George Washington Miller, a Confederate Army veteran, and who, after Col. Miller died, began the 101 Ranch Wild West Show. The 101 Ranch was a 110,000-acre cattle ranch and the largest diversified farm and ranch in America at the time. The year before, the Miller brothers had put on a show for the National Editorial Association meeting in Guthrie, Oklahoma. It was then that the famous photo of Geronimo driving a Locomobile while wearing a top hat was taken. After he appeared at the 101 Ranch in 1906, Apache tradition has it that Geronimo made a side trip to Chilocco, where his daughter Eva and grandson Thomas were attending school. There he met Robert for the first time and declared, no doubt much to Robert's delight, that the boy was his son.

Thereafter, Robert spent his summers at Fort Sill with his father, although they were not particularly close because of their years apart.[2] Geronimo, who then lived with his new wife, Azul, in Guydelkon's house, asked Daklugie to let the boy stay with him. Ramona agreed, and Robert lived with them for a while, until one day, without asking, he took Daklugie's prize racehorse and rode it to death. Daklugie asked Eugene Chihuahua if the boy could stay with him and his wife, Viola. Eugene

Geronimo at the 1905 Roosevelt inaugural, about a year before he met his son
Robert for the first time.
COURTESY OF MARINA AMARAL

and Viola agreed and took Robert into their home. They had no further trouble from him.

Robert Geronimo never returned to Chilocco after Geronimo died; instead he went to Carlisle Indian Industrial School. After several years at Carlisle, he returned to Mescalero, where his mother and stepfather still lived and where many of the Chiricahuas at Fort Sill had moved in 1913. Living at Mescalero, Robert married three times, was divorced once, and had children of his own who have carried on the family name.[3]

Geronimo's Power

THE APACHES BELIEVED IN ONE CREATOR GOD, USSEN, WHO CREATED and sent to earth White Painted Woman. She had two sons, Child of the Water and Killer of Enemies, who killed the giants terrorizing the earth. The Apaches believed Ussen gave special powers to individuals. Gifts of power were intended to be used for the good of the people, but the powers were morally neutral, neither good nor bad. These powers ranged across a wide range of capabilities, from performing healing ceremonies to sensing the direction from which enemies came to identifying witches and their power. To Apaches, the concept of a witch was a perfectly rational idea. A witch was one who was given special powers to help the people but instead used their gifts for evil and their own ends. Those caught practicing witchcraft were killed, usually by being burned alive, tied upside down to a wagon wheel with their heads over a slow fire. For the Apaches, fire was the only sure way to destroy evil.

The Apaches believed that anyone might receive a particular power and be called a *di-yen* (medicine man or woman). The Apaches believed gifts of power could come at any time and in a variety of ways, including through dramatic visions after a long period of fasting and self-denial, dreams, and flashes of insight. Power came suddenly and unexpectedly—as the life force of the universe seeking those through whom it might work—and it could come to men or women. Failure to use a gift of power meant it might be taken away.[1, 2]

One of the most famous Apache *di-yens* was Goyahkla (one who yawns), better known as Geronimo, the name his own people used. The historical record shows that Geronimo had powers such as seeing the future or events taking place far away, detecting the direction of enemies too far away to be seen, and carrying out healing ceremonies for his people.

C. D. Arnold photograph of Geronimo at the 1901 Pan-American Exposition in Buffalo, New York.

Geronimo acquired many kinds of power over the years. His first known gift of power came in 1850, while he and his family were camping with the Mangas Coloradas band and trading with the Mexicans near what is believed to be Janos (the Apaches called it Kas-ki-yeh), Chihuahua. The military commander in Sonora ignored the state boundary and peace agreement Chihuahua had with the Apaches and attacked the camp while the men were off in the village trading. Twenty-five Apaches, nearly all women and children, were killed, including Geronimo's mother, his first wife, and their three children all under the age of ten.

Short of warriors and weapons, Mangas Coloradas led the survivors on a tactical retreat back north until they could come again with enough strength and weapons to exact powerful revenge. During this time, Geronimo went out alone and sat with a flood of sorrow filling his eyes. He heard a voice call his name, "Goyahkla," four times, the magic number for Apaches. Then it said, "No gun can ever kill you. I'll take the bullets from the guns of the Mexicans, so they'll have nothing but powder. And I'll guide your arrows." The Mimbreños under the leadership of Mangas Coloradas, the Chiricahuas under Cochise, and the Nednhis under Juh went back to Arispe, Sonora, in the summer or late fall of the following year. The Apaches seemed to know that those who had ravaged their camp were stationed there. After some preliminary skirmishing the first day, there was a pitched battle the next day, which was not the usual Apache style of war fighting against two companies of cavalry and two of infantry. Because of his great loss of family members, Geronimo was allowed to direct the fighting. The battle lasted about two hours, with the Apaches fighting with bows and arrows and in close quarters with spears. Many were killed, but when the fight ended, the Apaches were still standing, and the Mexican companies were no more. According to tradition, this is where Goyahkla was given the name Geronimo.[3]

Twenty years later, Geronimo had another mountaintop experience. In the winter of 1869–1870, his sister (actually cousin) Ishton, beloved wife of Juh, was in hard labor to deliver her first child. Geronimo loved his sister and served as her *di-yen* during the delivery. She suffered terribly for four days. Geronimo believed she was going to die and that he had done all he knew to do for her. In distress, he climbed the mountain behind Fort

Bowie to pray to Ussen and ask for her life. As he stood praying with his arms and eyes raised, Ussen told him that his sister would live and promised him that he would never be killed but would live to a ripe old age and die a natural death. When he returned from the mountain, Ishton delivered a strong, healthy baby, Geronimo's nephew, Daklugie. Ishton lived to have yet another child, and Geronimo continued as a fearless warrior. His warriors were with him in many dangerous times and saw many miraculous escapes, his cures for wounds, and his medicine. They never doubted Geronimo had power from Ussen. In 1905, Geronimo showed his painter and friend Elbridge Ayer Burbank an astonishing number of scars on his body from bullet wounds, some large enough to hold small pebbles.

Geronimo had a gift for seeing the future or events far removed from where he was, and several witnesses saw this power. In 1883, General Crook with 193 scouts on foot, five packtrains of supplies and ammunition, and fifty mounted troopers disappeared into the Sierra Madre in Mexico to bring back the Apaches who had broken out of San Carlos and Fort Apache. Crook's scouts found one of the Apache camps high in the mountains near the headwaters of the Bavispe River. The scouts raided the camp, destroying supplies, taking prisoners, and killing a few who resisted. Crook ordered no more camp raids and sent survivors out to find the chiefs of other camps and ask that they come to him for talks. While this was going on, Geronimo and other warriors had been raiding for cattle in Sonora and were driving them back across the mountains to their camp. On the way, they stopped to rest and eat. The witnesses say that in the middle of a bite of beef Geronimo suddenly stopped, stared into space, and said something like, "Brothers! The Bluecoats are in our camps. What will we do?"[4] The warriors looked at each other in confusion as to what Geronimo meant. When they returned to their camps, they found the scouts and bluecoats waiting for them and their stores of meat, nuts, mescal, and berries for the winter destroyed.

The Apache leaders, facing a winter with little food, met with General Crook and discussed returning to San Carlos. They were disheartened because Crook's campaign had made them realize they could no longer raid in the United States and hide in Mexico with impunity and because Crook had found them by using scouts, their own people betraying their hiding places. All the leaders agreed to return to San Carlos with Crook's promise that their people would have a better place to live on the reservation. Leaders, including Naiche, Chihuahua, and Geronimo, told Crook that they would have to go and round up their people, who believed the smoke signals they saw to come in were from the scouts trying to catch them. Crook had little choice but to let them go.

When many of the leaders off looking for their people had not arrived by October, Crook sent Lt. Britton Davis to the border to look for them and escort them safely in. In late October, nearly five months after most of the Chiricahuas had returned to San Carlos, Naiche, with nine warriors and eighteen women and children, appeared at Davis's camp. Two weeks later, Chihuahua with his people came in, and others soon followed.

Geronimo did not come to San Carlos until late February. He had used the time well to gather about 350 head of cattle he had stolen from the Mexicans in order to start a Chiricahua herd at San Carlos. After avoiding a US marshal and a customs collector out to arrest Geronimo, Davis and Geronimo's people and cattle herd made it safely back to San Carlos. Unfortunately for Geronimo, Crook made him turn the stolen cattle over to the agency, which ultimately sold them and gave the proceeds to the Mexican government, which then had to sort out the claimants in Mexico. Twenty years later, Geronimo was still complaining about the cattle Crook had taken from him.

Geronimo was also given power and ceremonies to cure some physical and mental ailments. Even after Christianity had developed strong roots among the Fort Sill Chiricahuas, Geronimo continued to perform *di-yen* ceremonies for ghost sickness, coyote sickness, and a nervous disorder associated with touching a wolf. However, as more Chiricahuas became Christians, the number of requests for Geronimo's *di-yen* ceremonies declined, and believing his powers were in decline, he retreated to his village, rarely to be seen by most of the Chiricahuas.[5]

Geronimo lived on while others passed away. No doubt this raised suspicions about his being a witch, but he never considered that as a possibility for his life.[6] To Geronimo, whether Christian or follower of Apache beliefs about Ussen, power and its use was the center of his life.

Geronimo Looks For the Jesus Road

APACHES VIEWED THEIR SPIRITUAL LIVES AS INSEPARABLE FROM THEIR minute-to-minute physical lives. Thus, one of Geronimo's greatest struggles came when he looked for the Jesus road.

Under President U. S. Grant's Peace Policy, ministers and church members were to be selected as agents for the Indians. Particular denominations were selected and identified with each tribe. The Dutch Reformed Church, the Dutch branch of the Presbyterian Church, was selected for the Apaches. The church sent its first missionary, Choctaw minister Frank Hall Wright, a gifted evangelist, to the Indians in southwestern Oklahoma in 1895. However, the army wouldn't let him work with the recently arrived Apaches for about three years. When the army lifted its ban on missionaries approaching the Chiricahuas at Fort Sill, the commander replacing Captain Scott, Lt. Francis Henry Beach, allowed Wright and Dr. Walter C. Roe, who had established a mission among the Cheyenne, to call a council of the prisoners and present a plan for a mission. The council decided that the mission would focus on a school for the children, which would keep many of them from having to go away to the boarding school at Anadarko. Expressing the consensus of the group, Geronimo stood and said, "I, Geronimo, and these others are now too old to travel your Jesus road. But our children are young, and I and my brothers will be glad to have the children taught about the white man's God."[1]

With War Department permission, the mission buildings were built about two miles northwest of the post in a sheltered hollow the maps called the "Punch Bowl." The first building was a small frame schoolhouse. In August 1899 Maud Adkisson came as first mission worker and

J. W. Collins photograph of Geronimo in 1903, the year he found the Jesus road.

F. A. Moseley, as teacher. Anna Batey was hired as a kindergarten teacher when it was discovered that, in counting the children, about twenty-three kindergarteners had been overlooked. In the winter of 1899–1900, fifty-five to sixty children were enrolled in the school and, to the relief of their parents, weren't sent off to Anadarko. Older children were still sent away to boarding school, usually at Chilocco.

Reverend Wright and Dr. Roe started a Dutch Reformed church at the mission schoolhouse on September 30, 1900, with twenty-two members. Scout Noche was the first to join. Chihuahua, Chatto, and Naiche, whose commitment was so heartfelt that he changed his name to Christian Naiche and later named a son Christian, eventually followed him. There were also returning Carlisle students who had become Christians. These included Jason Betzinez, the Benedict Jozhes (a couple), James Kaywaykla and wife Dorothy Naiche, and Ramona Chihuahua, who was married to Daklugie, who, although not a member, always attended services with her. Zi-yeh, Geronimo's wife, had already embraced Christianity and was baptized through the Catholic Church.

Every summer, a camp meeting under a big tent was held on the mission grounds, and Indian families attending the daily services set up tents around it. Geronimo, seeing his influence as a *di-yen* slipping, retreated in silence to the village where he was headman and worked against the mission. At the camp meeting in the summer of 1902, Zi-yeh set up a tent, and Geronimo appeared on Sunday, the last day of the meeting.

Reverend Wright, learning that Geronimo had come, searched for and found him. After an earnest conversation, Geronimo promised to attend the night's services. At the service, he sat in the front row, motionless, with his hands folded in his lap. Near the end of the service, he jumped to his feet and made an impassioned speech, saying the Jesus road was best and ending with, "Now we begin to think that the Christian white people love us." The missionaries encouraged him but saw "a vein of self-importance in his talk" and did not then admit him to church membership.[2]

A year passed in which Geronimo went through periods of humility and gentleness and then arrogance and drinking. In July 1903, the camp meeting was held at the edge of the Punch Bowl among the oaks on

Medicine Bluff Creek. Earlier, Geronimo had been thrown from Zi-yeh's pony and badly hurt. Not present when services started in the morning, he came riding slowly, barely able to sit his horse, in the steamy afternoon. He entered the big tent, and Naiche went to him and sat down with him. Geronimo spoke in Apache to the group gathered around him, and Benedict Jozhe interpreted.

"He says he is in the dark. He knows that he is not on the right road and wants to find Jesus." Naiche's face was said to blaze with joy. In the days that followed, they explained to Geronimo what they believed and why.

At the last service, Geronimo accepted the faith. He said, "I'm old and broken by this fall I've had. I'm without friends, for my people have turned from me. I'm full of sins, and I walk alone in the dark. I see that you missionaries have got a better way to get sin out of the heart, and I want to take that better road and hold it till I die."[3]

Dr. Roe spoke privately with him and learned that Geronimo, despite appearances, had been listening carefully to what was being taught and learning from it. Geronimo was baptized a week later, and after the ceremony, Naiche embraced him, and women and children clung to his hands.

Two years later, Geronimo told S. M. Barrett, to whom he was dictating his autobiography, that he had always been religious and found much common ground between his old beliefs and the new ones. He didn't discard the beliefs he had lived by nearly all his adult life but supplemented them. He didn't find any difference between Christian worship and the sacred ceremonies of his people. This view was consistent with the belief of Father Braun, a Franciscan monk who ministered to the Mescaleros in the early to mid-twentieth century, but it was a much more liberal belief than that of the missionaries who had baptized Geronimo. Geronimo told Barrett, "I believe the Almighty has always protected me," which showed he still trusted the power Ussen had given him, although he expressed it as a Christian.[4]

For a while after his conversion, Geronimo's life appeared as pure as the driven snow, but he eventually couldn't resist the forbidden pleasures of feverish betting on horse races, gambling on any and everything, but especially cards, and a good, strong bottle of whiskey. Reverend Leonard L.

Legters, who became the church's minister in 1906 (and soon married the mission school's Maud Adkisson), pleaded with Geronimo to turn away from sliding back into sin. But Geronimo told Legters that the rules were "too strict," and he returned to the old beliefs of his fathers. In about 1907, he was suspended from membership in the church. As Angie Debo put it, "Throughout his life, Geronimo seemed to be all of one piece—a completely integrated personality—but it is clear that this religious episode brought a spiritual cleavage that was never closed. At the same time, his Power, the sustaining force of his long life, seemed to be breaking down."[5]

Geronimo Dictates His Autobiography

ONE DAY GERONIMO, SPEAKING SPANISH, WAS TRYING TO NEGOTIATE the sale of one of his war bonnets to an Anglo. The Anglo didn't understand Spanish, and the deal was going nowhere fast. S. M. Barrett, the Lawton school superintendent, was asked to help interpret Geronimo's Spanish on the price of the bonnet, and the deal was consummated. After that, Geronimo always had a friendly word for Barrett when they crossed paths.

Geronimo dictating his autobiography to S. M. Barrett, with Daklugie interpreting, ca. 1905.
COURTESY OF NATIONAL ARCHIVES

Geronimo learned that Barrett had once been wounded by a Mexican, so he visited him at his home and told Barrett of his hatred for Mexicans and its genesis. They became good friends and visited back and forth between their homes. A year later, in the summer of 1905 (after Geronimo had ridden in Theodore Roosevelt's inaugural parade), Barrett went to visit Geronimo at his house and brought along his friend Dr. J. M. Greenwood, superintendent of schools in Kansas City, Missouri. Geronimo was very formal around Dr. Greenwood until Greenwood said he was a friend of General Howard, whom he had heard speak of Geronimo. General Howard had negotiated the peace with Cochise in 1872, and Geronimo held him in high regard. Geronimo's whole demeanor changed, and he led Greenwood and Barrett to a shade tree, where he put on his war bonnet and served watermelon "Apache style," cut in big chunks, while he spoke freely and in good spirits.

Later in the summer, Barrett asked Geronimo to allow him to publish some of the stories that Geronimo had told him. Geronimo refused Barrett's proposal. However, he told Barrett that if he would pay him, and if officers in charge didn't object, he would tell him the entire story of his life. Without delay, Barrett went to Lt. George A. Purington, then in charge of the Apaches at Fort Sill, to request permission to write Geronimo's life story. Purington told Barrett not only no, but hell no, he would not be allowed to write Geronimo's story because of Geronimo's many depredations and the great expense it cost the army to stop them. If anything, he believed Geronimo deserved to be hanged rather than given such lavish attention by civilians. Barrett saw that suggesting the government had spent extraordinary sums of money for the army to stop marauding Apaches, and that the army had not been able to get the job done, wouldn't help the pride of working army officers. Barrett concluded he needed to find approval for his collaborative work at a higher level.

Barrett wrote a letter to President Theodore Roosevelt explaining that he wanted to give Geronimo (whom Roosevelt had met earlier that year during his inaugural parade, at which time he turned down Geronimo's request to return to the Arizona wilderness where he wanted to die) an opportunity to tell his side of his life's story and that the publication of the story would not affect the Apache prisoners of war unfavorably.

Barrett soon received a letter from Roosevelt that he had been granted authority to go forward with the project.

Within a few days, word came from Fort Sill announcing the president's approval and requesting that Barrett come for an interview with Lieutenant Purington to receive instructions from the War Department. Purington showed Barrett a list of ten endorsements by various officers in the War Department that said Purington was to be the army point of contact, that the manuscript should be reviewed for truthfulness, that Barrett would be held responsible for what was written and published, and that it was to be reviewed by any experts the secretary of war might choose.[1]

Geronimo wanted his nephew, Asa Daklugie, who had been educated at the Carlisle Indian school, to act as Barrett's interpreter, and Barrett was happy to use him. Daklugie didn't understand why Geronimo agreed to do the book. It wasn't the way the old Apaches preserved their history and traditions. The custom was for the older people to tell their stories repeatedly to the young ones while they sat around campfires and listened. However, Daklugie agreed to serve as the interpreter, trusting that crafty Geronimo, who had power to see the future, would keep them out of trouble.

There were many things Daklugie and Geronimo had to consider when telling his story to Barrett. First, they were prisoners of war and believed at the time that a change in military command might mean execution for all the prisoners; none of the prisoners had a sense of security, so nothing that was said could incriminate anyone else. (This was a common cultural view among the Apaches; even Apaches at Mescalero, for example, wouldn't acknowledge that relatives still lived in Mexico because they believed people looking for revenge might come after them.) Second, they thought Barrett might be a spy trying to get information that couldn't be found by any other means. Third, they knew Barrett had problems getting government consent for the project and had to get approval for the book from President Roosevelt. This suggested to them that the government wanted Geronimo to admit something. Daklugie and Geronimo discussed all these issues. Geronimo was shrewd and suspicious; he had greater supernatural power than Daklugie, and he could foresee what would happen. Daklugie decided to rely on Geronimo to keep them out of trouble. So the work began.[2]

Geronimo laid down a set of rules that Barrett and Daklugie had to follow as he told his story. Geronimo refused to talk when a stenographer was present or to wait for corrections or questions when he told his story. Each day that he spoke for the book, he had in mind what he would talk about, and he said it in a "very clear and brief manner" at some place he would designate, such as his home, Daklugie's place, out in the woods, or even riding horses across the plains. His directive was "Write what I have spoken," and they were to do this without questions, writing down what they remembered and without any other assistance. Geronimo did agree to come to any place Barrett designated to listen to his record of what he had been told, answer questions, and add any additional information.[3]

When word got out that Geronimo was dictating his life story, some of the younger men who had been with him at the surrender, influenced by scouts Noche and Chatto, became fearful that Geronimo would tell stories that would get them into trouble with the authorities, and they grew to dislike Geronimo as much as Noche and Chatto did. Geronimo knew this and was very careful not to implicate any of them. Daklugie and Kanseah (a young warrior, still loyal to Geronimo) believed this was the reason Lot Eyelash accused Geronimo of witching his children in order to live longer. Eyelash had never set himself up as a medicine man until then.[2]

Daklugie pointed out to Eve Ball, in telling her about the creation of the autobiography, that Geronimo was very careful about what he told Barrett and that he had been just as careful interpreting. Barrett couldn't do shorthand and only took notes. He couldn't write as fast as Daklugie talked, so he had to depend on his memory of what Daklugie told him. After the book was published, Daklugie often wondered if Barrett didn't try to make what Geronimo told him conform to what other books and military reports said. Nothing could have made Geronimo angrier. He knew (and most professional historians now know) how unreliable military reports could be, and he knew much that he didn't include in his story.

In discussing Barrett's work with Daklugie, Eve Ball pointed out that Barrett had written of Geronimo as a chief. Daklugie answered, "Well,

Geronimo never told him that. Neither did I. It was Barrett who made a chief of my uncle. As you know, Naiche was chief." When Ball remarked that there were other questionable statements in Barrett's Geronimo story, Daklugie answered, "I know, but Geronimo didn't put them there. Neither did I. Barrett either misunderstood or thought that Geronimo didn't know what he was talking about. There are many errors in that book. And Geronimo was far too wise to tell all he knew." Ball wrote that she made a mental note that Daklugie, too, knew what information to withhold.[2]

Geronimo the Witch

ONE BY ONE, GERONIMO HAD SEEN HIS FRIENDS AND WIVES PASS AWAY. As old age marched him toward his death, his possession of supernatural power began to cast a dark shadow in the eyes of the Apaches. They admired and trusted those who had power, but they feared its ultimate use. They believed that as death approached, the possessor of power might transfer its call to another person, especially a relative. As Geronimo continued to live while those he was close to, including his warrior friends, rode the ghost pony to the Happy Place, dark suspicions about what he might be doing to continue to live began to grow. Angie Debo pointed out that if he was aware of those suspicions, he never said so, and the idea of using his power to preserve his life seemed to have never entered his mind.[1]

Geronimo had seen more than his share of family deaths in his time. During his captivity, wives, children, and grandchildren fell like fruit dropping from the tree of life. When Chappo died from tuberculosis in Alabama, he was about thirty-one years old, and his wife and child died about the same time. Within five years of being transferred to Fort Sill, Geronimo's son Fenton, his daughter Dohn-say, and all her family, except her son Thomas, had passed away. Geronimo had strong feelings for his grandson Thomas. At the Chilocco Indian school, two hundred miles north of Fort Sill, Thomas was "a good student and worker," and as he grew into manhood, Geronimo's hopes increased that the boy would carry on the family name. Then, only eight months after Fenton died at age sixteen or seventeen, Thomas rode the ghost pony on March 11, 1908, at age eighteen, and the old man was devastated. He began to suspect someone with power was using an evil influence to destroy his family.

Geronimo, ca. 1906, two years before being accused of being a witch and killing off his children in order to continue living.
COURTESY OF LIBRARY OF CONGRESS

Eva began showing signs of some kind of lingering illness. Desperate to save his children, he became convinced that someone had "witched" Thomas and probably his other children as well. In 1908, less than a year before he died, he called for a dance to discover the witch. Lot Eyelash, who along with Chappo had been a novitiate with the warriors in the Sierra Madre during Geronimo's second breakout from San Carlos from 1881 to 1883, was to be in charge of the ceremony. After three or four songs, Lot Eyelash stopped the dancing and announced his findings. Looking at Geronimo, he pointed at him and yelled, "You did it! You did it so you could live on." Lot Eyelash was saying what many Apaches had suspected as Geronimo continued to outlive his family and friends. They believed he remained alive because he was using his power as a witch and offering others to death in his place while he stayed in the land of the living. When Geronimo heard this, he must have felt as though he had been burned with a hot knife.[1]

Probably this disaster in his faith led him to reconsider his belief in Christianity. He talked to the missionaries at the camp meeting that summer and said he wanted to start again, but he was also telling his friends he still believed in the old ways and enjoyed gambling and drinking. The missionaries told him he had to choose between their straight Jesus road and the road he then walked. Seven or eight months later, Geronimo enjoyed a good bottle of whiskey with his "grandson" Eugene Chihuahua in early February, caught pneumonia sleeping off the drunk in a cold winter rain, and died. In his fevered imaginings as his life left him, Geronimo saw Thomas and one of his friends, Nat Kayihtah, son of scout Kayihtah, who had also died, urging him to become a Christian. He told them he had been unable "to follow the path" in his life and asked why they had not come sooner. They answered that he had heard the missionaries and refused to listen to them; therefore, he would not listen to his vision either (which sounds remarkably like New Testament theology).

Geronimo's Last Two Wives, Sousche and Sunsetso

AFTER THE PASSING OF ZI-YEH, GERONIMO WAS CARED FOR BY HIS daughter Eva. Geronimo was old-school Apache. He expected to provide for a woman who would look after his household, and with Eva eligible for marriage, he probably felt he needed a wife in case Eva married, despite his refusal to approve her choice or any other eligible man for that matter.

Geronimo married again on Christmas Day 1905. The woman was an Apache named Sousche, or Mrs. Mary Loto.[1] According to newspaper accounts, she had been the widow of a "famous Indian" for two years and was the mother of one son. The marriage was not announced until around January 10, 1906, and came as a complete surprise even to close friends. The Chiricahuas at Fort Sill didn't know who Sousche was or where she came from. Speculation had it that since Mescaleros and others from tribes living around Fort Apache or San Carlos often visited the Chiricahuas at Fort Sill, Sousche was one of those people. Although by this time Geronimo was considered a Christian convert, he and Sousche didn't formalize their marriage through a Christian ceremony. Geronimo lived with Sousche for about three months before she left him, and by Apache custom they were then divorced. As Geronimo told Barrett, "Since the death of Eva's mother, I married another woman, but we couldn't live happily and separated. She went home to her people—that is an Apache divorce."

A year passed, and Geronimo took another wife. A Chiricahua widow called Sunsetso or Old Lady Yellow, but with the Spanish name

Geronimo and Sunsetso (aka Azul) ca. 1908.
COURTESY OF NATIONAL ARCHIVES

Azul (Blue), she was about twenty-five years younger than Geronimo. Why the colors in her names were different is not known. Azul looked after her two nearly grown grandnephews and Paul Guydelkon, the husband of her niece, who had passed away ten years earlier. She lived in Guydelkon's house in Perico's village, south of Geronimo's village and within easy walking distance.[2]

Azul had a son, Guy Amardo, before her husband died. Since she already lived with an established household, Geronimo moved in with her, just as he might have as a young man taking his first wife and joining her family.

Geronimo's marriage to Azul was apparently a happy one. As old age caught up with him, he began to go downhill physically and mentally in his last full year of life. He'd look for his hat when it was on his head or his knife when it was in his hand. Stories told by those who were around the couple hint that they teased each other about their frailties and stayed in good spirits.

In February 1909, Geronimo caught pneumonia after getting drunk and sleeping in a cold rain. Although many came to the hospital as he lay dying, only Azul and his "grandson" Eugene Chihuahua and "nephew" Asa Daklugie were with him until he breathed his last. After Geronimo left for the Happy Place, Azul had to be physically restrained from killing Geronimo's sorrel racing pony so he would have a ghost pony to ride. Azul moved to Mescalero with most of the other Chiricahuas in 1913 and never remarried.[3] She passed away at Mescalero in 1934 at about age eighty-four. Geronimo had been a lucky man to marry so well late in life.

Geronimo Rides the Ghost
Pony to the Happy Place

THE YEAR OF GERONIMO'S BIRTH IS UNCERTAIN. S. M. BARRETT IN
Geronimo's autobiography says it was 1829, but as a child, Geronimo
grew up with Jason Betzinez's mother, who remembered Halley's Comet
and "the Night the Stars Fell," which makes her birth year, which should
be about the same as Geronimo's, about 1823. Additionally, it is known
that he had a wife and three children by 1850 or earlier, which means if
he first married at seventeen and his oldest child was about ten (the old
Apaches spaced their children three or four years apart), this would again
place his birth year about 1823. Nevertheless, if Geronimo's birth year
is uncertain, it is certain his last months show a man in physical decline
fighting to live dreams filling him for over twenty years.

In the last two years of his life, Geronimo married a good woman,
Azul, who looked after him after he moved in with her. Living with Azul
and her grandnephews and her niece's widowed husband, Geronimo continued to make bows and arrows he autographed for sale to tourists who
came to Fort Sill or Lawton to see him.

By autumn of 1908, four or five months before he rode the ghost
pony to the Happy Place, Geronimo was not well. He had grown physically smaller, and his memory had become even poorer than it had been
a few months earlier. However, those who knew him also knew he still
had two dreams he longed to fulfill. The first dream was clear. He had
ridden in Theodore Roosevelt's 1905 inaugural parade with five of the
great chiefs from the plains and mountains Indian wars, and two days
later had eloquently petitioned Roosevelt to let him return to the place

Larry Smith's photograph of Geronimo's gravesite, Fort Sill, Oklahoma. His daughter Eva's grave is to the left; his wife Zi-yeh's grave is to the right. Other family members' graves are nearby. Geronimo's monument was built in 1928.
COURTESY OF NATIONAL ARCHIVES

of his birth on the headwaters of the Gila River near Clifton, Arizona. Roosevelt told Geronimo that he held nothing against him but couldn't let him return home because blood would surely flow, caused by those wanting revenge for the tragedies they had suffered in the Apache Wars. Nevertheless, Geronimo never lost an opportunity to ask again and again to return to the place of his birth, there to die an old man on his bed as Ussen had promised.

Geronimo's second dream appeared when it became clear that the peace terms General Miles had offered to get the Naiche-Geronimo band to surrender were empty promises at best and outright lies at worst. This led Geronimo to think often of Victorio's death. Geronimo had known Victorio at least from the time they had both led big raids south into Mexico under the direction of Mangas Coloradas, who was then unquestionably the most powerful Apache leader. Beginning in late August 1879, Victorio began a yearlong war on both sides of the border, leaving blood and fire wherever he went. Finally, in October 1880, Victorio, low on ammunition, camped at Tres Castillos and sent his segundo, Nana, out to find ammunition to resupply their weapons. While Nana was gone, Victorio was attacked by a large Mexican force led by Col. Joaquin Terrazas and in the following firefight quickly ran out of ammunition. Rather than be taken by the Mexicans, Victorio fired his last bullet and then stabbed himself in the heart. Near the end of his life, it became apparent that Geronimo much regretted that he had surrendered to General Miles. He told those close to him that he dreamed he had died fighting like Victorio, plunging his knife into his heart to avoid being taken by his enemies.

The two Geronimo dreams were constant, intertwined threads that ran throughout the years of his captivity. They were unfulfilled dreams because Geronimo had kept his part of the surrender terms.

In the second week of February 1909, Geronimo rode his sorrel racing pony to Lawton, where he sat outside a store most of a cold day and sold his signature bows and arrows to passersby. That afternoon he saw his "grandson" Eugene Chihuahua on the street and, giving him some money, asked Eugene to buy him some whiskey to warm his belly and to celebrate a good day of sales.

Selling whiskey to an Indian was a penitentiary offense. Eugene, a scout, was in his 7th Cavalry uniform, which fit so well he couldn't hide a bottle in or under his uniform coat. He gave the money to a friend, who bought a bottle for him and put it on the corner of a rail to which a picket fence was nailed that ran along the road next to the saloon. Eugene raced his pony past the fence, snatched the bottle, and headed out of town, soon joining Geronimo. They stopped along Cache Creek where there was some timber, watered the horses, and hobbled them in some good grass. They made a small fire and then drank the bottle dry between them. Geronimo probably drank most of it. Eugene, as an Indian scout in Gen. Armstrong Custer's old 7th Cavalry, knew he would be in big trouble if he were caught drunk.

What happened next is the subject of two conflicting stories. Angie Debo gives the most commonly known story in her excellent biography

Geronimo.[1] In this version, after drinking the whiskey, Geronimo tried to ride back home in the dark to Guydelkon's house, where he lived with his wife, Azul, in Perico's village. Nearly home, he fell off his horse next to a creek and lay there all night, partly in the creek and partly on the ground. At sunrise, Mrs. Jozhe saw the horse standing saddled on the bank of the creek, and she and others went to investigate. They found Geronimo and carried him to his house, where he was looked after for the next three days after contracting a severe cold that grew worse. After three days, a scout, probably Benedict Jozhe, reported that Geronimo was very ill to the post surgeon, who sent an ambulance to bring him to the little Apache hospital. But the ambulance detail found Geronimo surrounded by about a dozen women, including his wife, who refused to let him go. (The Apaches saw many go into the hospital alive only to come out dead.) The surgeon reported what had happened to Lieutenant Purington, the prisoners' army commander. Purington ordered an escorted detail to return and bring Geronimo to the hospital. By this time, Geronimo was suffering from pneumonia. It was Monday, February 15, 1909.

Eugene Chihuahua, who bought the whiskey for Geronimo, told the second version of the story to Eve Ball, and it is recorded in her oral history *Indeh*, written with Nora Henn and Lynda Sánchez.[2] According to Eugene, after he and Geronimo drank the whiskey, they went to sleep covered only by their saddle blankets. Toward morning, a cold, drizzling rain and Geronimo's coughing awakened Eugene. Eugene felt Geronimo's face, and it was hot. Geronimo told Eugene he had been sick all night but didn't disturb him because he thought the whiskey would make him better. Eugene saddled the horses and got him to the Apache hospital. The post surgeon examined Geronimo and said he had pneumonia. Eugene sent a man to tell Geronimo's wife, Azul. On her way to the hospital, Azul stopped and told Daklugie. Thereafter, it didn't take them long to get to the hospital.

Eugene stayed with Geronimo all that day, and Daklugie stayed that night. Daklugie and Eugene stayed with Geronimo around the clock in twelve-hour shifts, never leaving him alone. Many people came to the hospital, but the nurses would only let Azul, Daklugie, and Eugene into the room. Both Daklugie and Eugene made medicine for him, Daklugie using Apache Ussen ceremonies and Eugene praying to the Christian God. The post surgeon gave Geronimo the best White Eye medicine, but nothing did any good. It was Geronimo's time. Geronimo knew this and asked that his beloved daughter Eva and his recently discovered son Robert be brought to the hospital so he could see them one last time. He was determined to live until they came. Unfortunately, Lieutenant Purington sent Eva and Robert a letter rather than a telegram, telling them they needed to come as soon as possible. Thus, they didn't arrive for two days.

Geronimo died at 6:15 a.m. on February 17, 1909. Men had to stop Azul from killing his sorrel racing pony for him to ride to the Happy Place. All day long, grieving old women passed through the little stone building where his body lay, and somber, dry-eyed men stood outside watching.

Geronimo's funeral was scheduled for February 18 at 3:00 p.m. The procession to the cemetery was delayed until Eva and Robert arrived, grief-stricken, on the train a little after 3 p.m. It is said that the procession was nearly a mile long and included virtually the entire Apache tribe, most of the Anglos in Lawton, and Fort Sill soldiers who had been given a half day off to attend the funeral.

Naiche stood at the graveside and gave Geronimo's eulogy in Apache. Eugene Chihuahua served as interpreter for the formal service conducted by Rev. Leonard Legters.

Geronimo was buried with his greatest treasures. Daklugie told Eve Ball that two Apaches stood guard over the grave every night for months to ensure the grave was not dug up and the treasures stolen and that Geronimo's head wasn't taken for his skull, as had happened to Mangas Coloradas, whose corpse was dug up and decapitated, with the skull being sent to the Smithsonian Institution. Time passed, and as there was no attempt to molest Geronimo's grave, guard duty was reduced to two nights a week.

A report came that the body had been dug up and decapitated—by Apaches.[2] Two men were under suspicion. They were watched for years because if they were guilty, they would have to sell the loot to make any money. According to Daklugie, as far as anyone knew, the men never came into any unexpected money. The Apaches had expected that the ghouls who had stolen the skull of Geronimo would carry it around the country and put it on display for the price of a ticket, but that never happened. In 1928, the army covered the grave with a slab of concrete and placed a piled-stone monument with an eagle on top to commemorate Geronimo's burial place.

For several years, a rumor persisted that in 1918 six army officers (including Prescott Bush, grandfather of George W. Bush), who were graduates of Yale University, had broken into the grave and taken the skull, femur bones, and other artifacts and sent them to their Skull and Bones society in New Haven, Connecticut. The story gained momentum in 2005 when Marc Wortman, researching a book about Yale army officer flyers in World War I, discovered a letter in a Yale library that referred to the theft. In 2009, Apaches brought a lawsuit to have the skull and other artifacts returned to the grave. The lawsuit was thrown out on a couple of technicalities. The plaintiff's lawyer, Ramsey Clark, admitted he had no hard evidence, and the Skull and Bones society swore it did not have the skull or any artifacts. No independent evidence has been found that Geronimo's grave was disturbed in 1918.

In fact, the letter Wortman uncovered suggests the Yale-educated officers who purportedly dug up the skull invaded the wrong grave. When the grave was disturbed in 1918, Geronimo's grave had only a simple army-issue wooden headstone marker, like that of the other Apaches buried at Fort Sill. The letter Wortman uncovered includes lines that read, "The ring of pick on stone and thud of earth on earth alone disturbs the peace of the prairie. An axe pried open the iron door of the tomb, and Pat Bush entered and started to dig." The letter goes on to say the officers closed the grave, shut the iron door, and sped home to Pat Mallon's room, where they cleaned the bones.

There was no stone or iron door associated with the grave of Geronimo at that time. Furthermore, the Apache prisoner of war cemetery was three miles away from Fort Sill across swampy prairie, and the bridge to get there was often out. In fact, many Apaches didn't know where the cemetery was in 1918. However, in the old post near the quadrangle is the easily accessible Fort Sill Cemetery. There, next to the marker for Quanah Parker, is a waist-high, stonewalled tomb for the Kiowa chief

Kicking Bird. It has a small iron door with a latch that can be pried open with an axe. Based on these facts and other pertinent information, retired history professor David Miller made a persuasive argument that the well-educated Yale army officers in the Order of Skull and Bones in fact went to the wrong cemetery, went to the wrong grave, and took the skull of the wrong warrior, the Kiowa Kicking Bird.[3] It appears Geronimo, once a master at disappearing from enemies, had the last laugh on the Order of Skull and Bones. Rest in peace, Geronimo.

EPILOGUE

IN THE LAST YEAR OF GERONIMO'S LIFE, THE PRESSURE INCREASED FROM military officers, philanthropic Indian associations, and Chiricahua leaders, including Geronimo, to free the Chiricahuas as prisoners of war. Geronimo wanted to go back to his birthplace to finish out his life, but everyone from President Theodore Roosevelt to army generals to Bureau of Indian Affairs bureaucrats had determined that would never happen. A month or two before Geronimo died, Daklugie paid for his travel to visit bureaucrats in Washington to ask that his people be released. He then journeyed to Mescalero in south-central New Mexico to look over the reservation in order to determine if there was enough land and grass to support the Chiricahuas who wanted to move there. Happy with what he saw, he returned to Fort Sill to report his impression that the reservation was a fine place for the Chiricahuas to settle and that the Mescaleros had told him they would welcome them when the Chiricahuas were freed.

After Geronimo died, there was little doubt in any quarter that the Chiricahuas would be freed. The army had decided it wanted to keep the Fort Sill land to use for an artillery school, which meant the Chiricahuas had to give up the land in which they had invested eighteen years raising families, building houses, planting crops, stringing miles of fence, growing one of the best cattle herds in the state, and burying loved ones who had passed away, mostly from White Eye diseases. They would have to start over again, as they had when they were promised they would be given land at Fort Sill.

The wheels of bureaucracy turned slowly. Four years after Geronimo died in 1909, the internment of Chiricahua Apaches as prisoners of war ended for those going to Mescalero. Those who stayed were released a year later in 1914. During those years, Geronimo's last child, Eva, and her baby passed away. The only known survivors among Geronimo's children, Lenna and Robert, grew up on the Mescalero reservation and didn't fall victim to the diseases or warfare that killed the rest of their brothers and sisters. They were alive because Geronimo had chosen to sacrifice his marriage to Ih-tedda in order to save his wife and child from living in the death trap prisoner of war camps.

When it was finally decided to free the Chiricahuas, they were given the choice of staying on individual farms near Fort Sill or moving to the Mescalero reservation in the Sacramento Mountains in south-central New Mexico. Daklugie and Eugene Chihuahua believed Mescalero was the best place for their families, and the majority of the Chiricahuas joined them.

The Mescaleros welcomed 183 (70 percent) of the Chiricahuas to their reservation. Among them were Geronimo's last wife, Azul; her grandnephew Paul Guydelkon and his father; Geronimo's "nephew" Asa Daklugie and his family; and Geronimo's "grandson" Eugene Chihuahua.

The Chiricahuas established their homes and a cattle herd in the White Tail area on the reservation. The herd became the envy of ranchers everywhere in New Mexico. Initially, the Chiricahuas lived in large army tents with vertical walls they reinforced with brush and dirt. They cut wood for iron stoves to keep the winter cold out. After their arrival, they began asking the Mescalero agent C. R. Jefferis for materials to begin building comfortable houses like the ones they had in Oklahoma. Jefferis immediately requested funds from the Bureau of Indian Affairs. After filling out reams of paperwork and waiting four years for the bureaucrats to make up their minds, Jefferis, in disgust, sold some reservation timber and bought what the Chiricahuas needed to build their houses.

Seventy-eight Chiricahuas stayed behind in Oklahoma. Government representatives purchased farms for them in the rich agricultural land about twenty miles northwest of Fort Sill and centered on the town of Apache. Each had been promised 160 acres for ranching or 80 acres for farming; most were lucky to get a total of 80 acres for ranching and 40 acres for farming. In many ways, those staying in Oklahoma had to adjust to a more difficult lifeway than their brothers who went to Mescalero. Those who stayed had to support themselves with farming and trades and to forge social relationships in a predominantly white society.

Years later, Daklugie, a leader of the Chiricahuas at Mescalero, told chronicler Eve Ball,

> *Eugene and I are largely responsible for bringing our people here. At the time we did it, we did not have the wisdom to know that we were making a terrible mistake. We thought that we had made the right decision. We had no alternative except that of staying in Oklahoma and becoming farmers. No Apache really wanted to farm; but those who did were better off than the ones who came to this reservation. Why? Because those at Fort Sill became dependent on themselves by the farming experience, and they seemed to have been strengthened. While it is true we were in captivity in Oklahoma, it was an entirely different type of supervision. The Apaches will tell you that they did better under military control than under civilian administration. The officers at Fort Sill had wisely left both the management and decisions largely up to the chiefs or headmen, each of whom had a village. Their primary functions were to maintain order and standards. It is different at Mescalero, even though it is perhaps the richest in natural resources of any [reservation] in the United States.*

Geronimo's passing marked the end of an era across a time of great change. Geronimo was an "old" Apache. He was born with a burning desire to live free. His life was infused with tribal culture, customs, and beliefs, and he placed great value on and sacrificed anything for his family. He believed the Apache creator god, Ussen, had given him great and powerful spiritual gifts, making him a *di-yen*, a medicine man for his people. He was a warrior and a war leader. Wounded many times, he survived to fight another day. He was tactically brilliant, his charisma as a war leader was powerful, his fighting skills were unquestioned, and in his later years, his thirst for revenge against Mexicans was unslakable. Geronimo was a hard-eyed killer. His small, black eyes burned with a fierce light that counted friends and enemies. Near the end of his life, he often regretted he had surrendered and not fought to his last bullet and then killed himself.

After agreeing to surrender terms that were never honored, Geronimo still kept his word and lived with his people as a prisoner of his captor's lies for the remaining twenty-three years of his life. In that time, he became nationally famous and a mythical hero. He saw two wives, two grown children, and four grandchildren die from White Eye diseases. Beginning near age sixty-five, he married twice, divorced twice, and fathered two children. He knew Ussen, as the Apaches knew him, and he knew the God the White Eyes said was the one, true God. Through a hard, selfless choice on his part, two of his children survived to carry on his bloodline. The descendants of those children live today in the Sacramento Mountains of New Mexico, proud of their family names and that of their great-great-grandfather.

Today the wind whispers through the trees and over the monument covering Geronimo's grave on the Oklahoma prairie far from the land of his birth. And sometimes, if you listen carefully, you might hear music, a song Geronimo often sang resting on his bed or riding his pony.

> *O, ha le*
> *O, ha le*
> *Through the air*
> *I fly upon a cloud*
> *Toward the sky, far, far, far*
> *O, ha le*
> *O, ha le*
> *There to find the holy place*
> *Ah, now the change comes o'er me*
> *O, ha le*
> *O, ha le.*

Notes

Prologue

1. Most of the historical information recorded here comes from *Geronimo*, by Angie Debo.
2. *Indeh*, by Eve Ball, Nora Henn, and Lynda Sánchez, pp. 20–21.
3. *Apache Odyssey: A Journey Between Two Worlds*, by Morris Opler, pp. 154–163.
4. *Geronimo's Story of His Life*, by Geronimo and S. M. Barrett.
5. *The Apache Rock Crumbles*, by Woodward B. Skinner.
6. *The Chiricahua Apache Prisoners of War: Fort Sill, 1894–1914*, by John Anthony Turcheneske Jr.

Part I: Surrender
Geronimo's Relationship with Naiche

1. *Geronimo*, by Angie Debo.
2. *Indeh*, by Eve Ball, Nora Henn, and Lynda Sánchez.
3. Ibid., p. 136.
4. *Apache Agent*, by John Clum, pp. 272–276.
5. Debo, p. 283.
6. Debo, p. 442.
7. *Apache Voices*, by Sherry Robinson, p. 58.

Geronimo's Last Warriors

1. *Geronimo*, by Angie Debo, pp. 304–306.
2. *From Fort Marion to Fort Sill*, by Alicia Delgadillo with Miriam A. Perrett.

Lieutenant Charles B. Gatewood, the Bluecoat Geronimo Trusted

1. *Geronimo*, by Angie Debo, pp. 269–271.
2. *Indeh*, by Eve Ball, Nora Henn, and Lynda Sánchez, p. 82.
3. *Lt. Charles Gatewood and His Apache Wars Memoir*, edited with additional text by Louis Kraft, pp. 121–123.
4. Ibid., p. 124.
5. Ibid., p. 161.
6. Ibid., p. 162.

The Decision to Surrender
1. Most of the historical information recorded here comes from "Account of the Surrender of Geronimo," by Charles B. Gatewood, Tucson, Arizona Historical Society, Gatewood Collection, Manuscript, 1895.
2. *A Chiricahua Apache's Account*, by Morris Opler, pp. 375–377.
3. *Geronimo*, by Angie Debo, p. 292.
4. Ibid., pp. 256–257.
5. *The Apache Rock Crumbles*, by Woodward B. Skinner, p. 71.

The Apache Prisoner of War Train Stops in San Antonio
1. Most of the historical information recorded here comes from *Geronimo*, by Angie Debo, pp. 301–308.
2. See *Prisoner of Lies* chapter titled "Geronimo's Last Warriors" in Part I.

The Last Apaches to Surrender in 1886
1. *Geronimo*, by Angie Debo, p. 242.
2. *Indeh*, by Eve Ball, Lynda Sánchez, and Nora Henn, pp. 115–119.
3. Ibid., p. 117.

PART II: APACHE PRISONERS OF WAR IN FLORIDA AND CARLISLE, PENNSYLVANIA
Life at Fort Marion, Saint Augustine, Florida
1. According to Jason Betzinez in *I Fought with Geronimo*, p. 146, the people of Saint Augustine were friendly and sympathetic.
2. Most of the historical information recorded here comes from *The Apache Rock Crumbles*, by Woodward B. Skinner, pp. 119–123.
3. *Geronimo*, by Angie Debo, pp. 313–317.

First Days of Apache Children at Carlisle
1. Most of the historical information recorded here comes from *Indeh*, by Eve Ball, Nora Henn, and Lynda Sánchez, p. 136.
2. Ibid., pp. 140–145.

Student Life at Carlisle
1. *The Mescalero Apaches*, by C. L. Sonnichsen, pp. 252–253.
2. Most of the information here was told to Eve Ball by Daklugie, who was forced to attend Carlisle, and was recorded in *Indeh*, by Eve Ball, Lynda Sánchez, and Nora Henn, pp. 141–159.
3. Ibid., pp. 150–151.

Apache Prisoner of War Life at Fort Pickens, Pensacola, Florida
1. *The Apache Rock Crumbles*, by Woodward B. Skinner, p. 104–107.
2. *Geronimo*, by Angie Debo, pp. 309–310.
3. Ibid., pp. 321–323.

PART III: PRISONERS AT MOUNT VERNON BARRACKS, ALABAMA
Apache Prisoner of War Life at Mount Vernon Barracks
1. Most of the historical information recorded here comes from an oral history given by Eugene Chihuahua to Eve Ball and recorded in *Indeh*, by Eve Ball, Nora Henn, and Lynda Sánchez, pp. 152–159.
2. *Geronimo*, by Angie Debo, pp. 336–357.

Geronimo's Wives
1. The photo identified as Zi-yeh and son Fenton has also been identified as a wife named Taayzslath, and the photo is thought to have been taken ca. 1884, with the child identified as a daughter. However, Alicia Delgadillo and Miriam A. Perret in *From Fort Marion to Fort Sill* clearly describe Taayzslath and Zi-yeh as being one and the same person with the same children and years of birth and death. It is assumed here that Taayzslath and Zi-yeh are the same person and the child in the photograph is Fenton.
2. *Geronimo*, by Angie Debo, p. 469.
3. Delgadillo and Perrett, p. 159.
4. *Indeh*, by Eve Ball, Nora Henn, and Lynda Sánchez, p. 46.
5. Delgadillo and Perrett, p. 244.

Geronimo, Mount Vernon Barracks Schoolmaster
1. *Geronimo*, by Angie Debo, p. 339.
2. Ibid., pp. 340–341.
3. *Indeh*, by Eve Ball, Nora Henn, and Lynda Sánchez, p. 154.

General Crook's 1890 Mount Vernon Barracks Visit
1. Most of the historical information recorded here comes from *Geronimo*, by Angie Debo, pp. 344–347.
2. Senate Executive Document 35, 51st Congress, 1st Session, pp. 29–36.

Apache Prisoners of War Become an Army Unit
1. Debo, pp. 346–347.
2. Most of the historical information recorded here comes from *Geronimo*, by Angie Debo, pp. 349–350.
3. *The Apaches: Eagles of the Southwest*, by Donald E. Worcester, p. 319.

Geronimo Counsels Corporal Fun and His Wife
1. Most of the historical information recorded here comes from *The Apache Rock Crumbles*, by Woodward B. Skinner, pp. 326–328.
2. *Geronimo*, by Angie Debo, p. 354.
3. *From Fort Marion to Fort Sill*, by Alicia Delgadillo and Miriam A. Perrett.

The Apaches March to Mobile and Back
1. Most of the historical information recorded here comes from *The Apache Rock Crumbles*, by Woodward B. Skinner, pp. 328–333.
2. Ibid., p. 333.

George Wratten, Friend of the Chiricahuas
1. *The Apache Rock Crumbles*, by Woodward B. Skinner, p. 63.
2. Ibid., p. 64.
3. *Geronimo*, by Angie Debo, p. 304.
4. *Indeh*, by Eve Ball, Nora Henn, and Lynda Sánchez, p. 166.

Geronimo Tries to Fire George Wratten
1. Most of the historical information recorded here comes from *The Apache Rock Crumbles*, by Woodward B. Skinner, pp. 369–372.
2. Ibid., p. 370.
3. Ibid., p. 372.

Chiricahua Prisoners Make Their Case for a Move, August 29, 1894
1. Most of the historical information recorded here comes from *Geronimo*, by Angie Debo, pp. 360–363.

PART IV: PRISONERS OF WAR AT FORT SILL, OKLAHOMA
The Chiricahua Prisoners of War Go to Fort Sill, Oklahoma
1. Most of the historical information recorded here comes from *Geronimo*, by Angie Debo, pp. 363–370.
2. *Indeh*, by Eve Ball, Nora Henn, and Lynda Sánchez, p. 160.

Apache Prisoner of War Life at Fort Sill
1. Most of the historical information recorded here comes from *Geronimo*, by Angie Debo, pp. 372–378.
2. *Indeh*, by Eve Ball, Nora Henn, and Lynda Sánchez, pp. 160–164.
3. *The Apache Rock Crumbles*, by Woodward B. Skinner, pp. 397–398.

Geronimo on the Army Payroll
1. *Geronimo*, by Angie Debo, p. 354.
2. *Indeh*, by Eve Ball, Nora Henn, and Lynda Sánchez, p. 161.

Eldridge Ayer Burbank Paints Geronimo
1. Most of the historical information recorded here comes from *Geronimo*, by Angie Debo, pp. 379–386.
2. *Burbank Among the Indians*, by E. A. Burbank and Ernest Royce, pp. 32–33.

The Chiricahua Breakout Panic at Fort Sill
1. *The Chiricahua Apache Prisoners of War*, by John Anthony Turcheneske Jr., pp. 69–70.
2. *The Apache Rock Crumbles*, by Woodward B. Skinner, p. 406.

Geronimo Escapes!
1. *Geronimo*, by Angie Debo, pp. 406–407.
2. Ibid., pp. 425–426.

Geronimo, Superstar
1. See the figure with the chapter titled "The Apache Prisoner of War Train Stops in San Antonio" in *Prisoner of Lies*, Part I.
2. *Geronimo*, by Angie Debo, p. 405.
3. Ibid., pp. 409–417.
4. *Geronimo's Story of His Life*, by Geronimo and S. M. Barrett, pp. 197–206.
5. *Indeh*, by Eve Ball, Nora Henn, and Lynda Sánchez, p. 262.

Geronimo at the Saint Louis Louisiana Purchase Exposition
1. Most of the historical information recorded here comes from *Geronimo's Story of His Life*, by Geronimo and S. M. Barrett, pp. 197–206.
2. *Geronimo*, by Angie Debo, pp. 409–417.
3. *Indeh*, by Eve Ball, Nora Henn, and Lynda Sánchez, p. 262.

Geronimo's Contemporaries: The Great Chiefs
1. Most of the historical information recorded here comes from *Geronimo*, by Angie Debo, pp. 417–419.
2. *Indeh*, by Eve Ball, Nora Henn, and Lynda Sánchez, pp. 176–177.
3. Debo, pp. 38–40.
4. *Apache Voices*, by Sherry Robinson, pp. 65–78.

Geronimo's Children

1. *Geronimo*, by Angie Debo, p. 9.
2. *Indeh*, by Eve Ball, Nora Henn, and Lynda Sánchez, p. 62.
3. *From Fort Marion to Fort Sill*, by Alicia Delgadillo and Miram A. Perrett, pp. 94–95.
4. Debo, pp. 412–414.
5. Ball, p. 263.

Eva Geronimo

1. *Geronimo*, by Angie Debo, p. 355.
2. See *Prisoner of Lies* chapters titled "Apache Prisoner of War Life" and "Apache Prisoner of War Life at Fort Sill."
3. Debo, pp. 392–393.
4. *Indeh*, by Eve Ball, Nora Henn, and Lynda Sánchez, p. 181.

Robert, the Son Geronimo Didn't Know He Had

1. See *Prisoner of Lies* chapter titled "Geronimo's Children."
2. *Geronimo*, by Angie Debo, p. 397.
3. *From Fort Marion to Fort Sill*, by Alicia Delgadillo and Miram A. Perrett, pp. 96–97.

Geronimo's Power

1. Most of the historical information recorded here comes from *Geronimo's Story of His Life*, by Geronimo and S. M. Barrett, pp. 3–11.
2. *Geronimo*, by Angie Debo, p. 37.
3. Ibid, pp. 38–39.
4. *I Fought with Geronimo*, by Jason Betzinez, p. 113.
5. Debo, pp. 434–435.
6. See *Prisoner of Lies* chapter titled "Geronimo the Witch."

Geronimo Looks For the Jesus Road

1. *Geronimo*, by Angie Debo, p. 428.
2. Ibid., p. 431.
3. Ibid., p. 432.
4. *Geronimo's Story of His Life*, by Geronimo and S. M. Barrett, pp. 207–212.
5. Debo, pp. 435–436.

Geronimo Dictates His Autobiography

1. *Geronimo's Story of His Life*, by Geronimo and S. M. Barrett, pp. xi–xxvii.
2. *Indeh*, by Eve Ball, Nora Henn, and Lynda Sánchez, pp. 173–174.
3. *Geronimo*, by Angie Debo, pp. 390–391.

Geronimo the Witch
1. *Geronimo,* by Angie Debo, p. 437.

Geronimo's Last Two Wives, Sousche and Sunsetso
1. *Geronimo,* by Angie Debo, pp. 391–392.
2. Ibid., p. 397.
3. *From Fort Marion to Fort Sill,* by Alicia Delgadillo and Miram A. Perrett, p. 242.

Geronimo Rides the Ghost Pony to the Happy Place
1. *Geronimo,* by Angie Debo, p. 440.
2. *Indeh,* by Eve Ball, Nora Henn, and Lynda Sánchez, pp. 179–182.
3. Retired history professor David Miller, in a paper he has delivered in several venues, makes a persuasive argument based on these facts and others that Geronimo's grave was mistakenly not disturbed by officers from the Order of Skull and Bones in 1918. See the June 30, 2009, *Santa Fe Reporter* article titled "The Strange Saga of Geronimo's Skull" by Leo W. Banks.

Additional Reading
and Information Resources

Adams, David Wallace. *Education for Extinction*. Lawrence: University Press of Kansas, 1995.

Ball, Eve. *In the Days of Victorio: Recollections of a Warm Springs Apache*. Tucson: University of Arizona Press, 1970.

Ball, Eve, Nora Henn, and Lynda A. Sánchez. *Indeh: An Apache Odyssey*. Norman: University of Oklahoma Press, 1988.

Barrett, S. M. *Geronimo, His Own Story: The Autobiography of a Great Patriot Warrior*. New York: Meridian, Penguin Books USA, 1996.

Debo, Angie. *Geronimo: The Man, His Time, His Place*. Norman: University of Oklahoma Press, 1976.

Delgadillo, Alicia, with Miriam A. Perrett. *From Fort Marion to Fort Sill: A Documentary History of the Chiricahua Prisoners of War, 1886–1913*. Lincoln: University of Nebraska Press, 2013.

Gatewood, Charles B. *Lt. Charles Gatewood and His Apache Wars Memoir*, edited and additional text by Louis Kraft. Lincoln: University of Nebraska Press, 2005.

Haley, James L. *Apaches: A History and Culture Portrait*. Norman: University of Oklahoma Press, 1981.

Hutton, Paul Andrew. *The Apache Wars*. New York: Crown Publishing Group, 2016.

Opler, Morris, Edward. "A Chiricahua Apache's Account of the Geronimo Campaign of 1886," *New Mexico Historical Review* 13, no. 4 (October 1938).

———. *An Apache Life-Way: The Economic, Social, and Religious Institutions of the Chiricahua Indians*. Lincoln: University of Nebraska Press, 1996.

———. *Apache Odyssey: A Journey Between Two Worlds*. Lincoln: University of Nebraska Press, 2002.

Robinson, Sherry. *Apache Voices: Their Stories of Survival as Told to Eve Ball*. Albuquerque: University of New Mexico Press, 2003.

Scott, Hugh Lenox. *Sign Talker: Hugh Lenox Scott Remembers Indian Country*, edited by R. Eli Paul. Norman: University of Oklahoma Press, 2016.

Skinner, Woodward B. *The Apache Rock Crumbles*. Pensacola, FL: Skinner Publications, 1987.

Sonnichsen, C. L. *The Mescalero Apaches*. Norman: University of Oklahoma Press, 1973.

Stockel, H. Henrietta. *Shame and Endurance: The Untold Story of the Chiricahua Apache Prisoners of War*. Tucson: University of Arizona Press, 2004.

———. *Survival of the Spirit: Chiricahua Apaches in Captivity*. Reno: University of Nevada Press, 1993.

Sweeney, Edwin. *From Cochise to Geronimo: The Chiricahua Apaches, 1874–1886*. Norman: University of Oklahoma Press, 2010.

Thrapp, Dan L., *The Conquest of Apacheria*. Norman: University of Oklahoma Press, 1967.

Turcheneske, John Anthony Jr. *The Chiricahua Apache Prisoners of War: Fort Sill, 1894–1914*. Niwot: University Press of Colorado, 1997.

Utley, Robert M. *Geronimo*. New Haven, CT: Yale University Press, 2012.

Worchester, Donald E. *The Apaches: Eagles of the Southwest*. Norman: University of Oklahoma Press, 1992.

INDEX

(Note photos are indicated by *italics*)

About the Author

W. Michael Farmer combines ten plus years of research into nineteenth-century Apache history and culture with Southwest living experience to fill his stories with a genuine sense of time and place. He is a retired PhD physicist whose scientific research has included measurement of atmospheric aerosols with laser-based instruments, and he has published a two-volume reference book on atmospheric effects on remote sensing. He has also written short stories for anthologies and award-winning essays. His first novel, *Hombrecito's War*, won a Western Writers of America Spur Finalist Award for Best First Novel in 2006 and was a New Mexico Book Award Finalist for Historical Fiction in 2007. His other novels include *Hombrecito's Search*; *Tiger, Tiger, Burning Bright: The Betrayals of Pancho Villa*; and *Conspiracy: The Trial of Oliver Lee and James Gililland*. His *Killer of Witches: The Life and Times of Yellow Boy, Mescalero Apache, Book 1* won a Will Rogers Medallion Award and was a New Mexico–Arizona Book Awards Finalist in 2016. *Mariana's Knight: The Revenge of Henry Fountain* won the 2017 New Mexico–Arizona Book Award for Historical Fiction, and *Blood of the Devil: The Life and Times of Yellow Boy, Mescalero Apache, Book 2* was a finalist. These two novels have also won 2018 Will Rogers Awards. *Apacheria: True Stories of Apache Culture, 1860–1920* won the 2018 New Mexico–Arizona Book Awards for History—Other (other than New Mexico or Arizona) and for Best 2018 New Mexico Book.